RUNNING AFTER 40

by the editors of Runner's World Magazine

WORLD

World Publications, Inc.
Mountain View, California

Library of Congress Cataloging in Publication Data
Main entry under title:

Running after forty.

    1. Running. 2. Jogging. 3. Walking. 4. Middle
age. I. Runner's world.
Gv1061.R834 1979   796.4'26   78-68620
ISBN 0-89037-205-5 pbk.

Photo Credits

Foreword, Fionnbar Callanan; p. 9, David Madison; p. 13, Roderick Lum; p. 18, Jim Engle; p. 21, Jeff Kroot; p. 22, Jeff Johnson; p. 42, David Madison; p. 61, Joe Neil; p. 63, Vanucci Services; pp. 76-80, Jeff Reinking; p. 83, Steve Sutton; pp. 85, 86, & 102, Stan Pantovic; p. 108, Omphoto; p. 116, Jeff Reinking; p. 125, Kathrine Switzer; p. 128, Jim Engle; p. 131, Lorraine Rorke; p. 134, Action Photos; p. 138, Jeff Johnson.

© 1980 by
World Publications, Inc.

World Publications, Inc.
Mountain View, CA

Contents

A regular program of long-distance running helps preserve muscular strength and endurance; maintains the strength of heart contractions; preserves blood vessel passageways; enhances circulation to the brain, skin, muscles, and endocrine glands; stimulates beneficial secretions of various hormones; promotes a healthful low blood pressure; prevents obesity; preserves bone strength; stimulates intestinal motility (preventing constipation); and promotes emotional tranquility and mental alertness. It is likely that running, with such profound and wide-ranging effects, moreso than any diet or drugs, will greatly prolong Man's life span.

—Fred E. Abbo, M.D., Ph.D.

Foreword

How Old Would You Be?
Joe Henderson

Satchel Paige pitched major league baseball when his age was somewhere between the late forties and early sixties. He either wasn't sure how old he was or wasn't telling.

Paige coined homespun philosophies that outlived his playing career. He's best known as the man who warned us not to look back: someone might be gaining on us.

Once, when asked the inevitable question about his age, Satchel answered with a question of his own: "How old would you be if you didn't know how old you were?"

Think about that. If you didn't know the year you were born, how old would you judge yourself to be by looks and feelings. There is no more accurate test than that. We can't tell by looking at teeth as we would with a horse, or by sawing ourselves in half and counting rings as with a tree.

If you asked me Paige's question, I would say, "It depends. How old *where?*" Like all of us, I'm a man of many ages.

As an athlete, I'm almost ancient. Thirteen years ago, someone asked me, "What's an old guy like you doing still running?" And I'm *still* running.

As a writer, I'm a child. Everywhere I go to meet readers, someone says, "I expected someone older"—as if gray hair is a qualification for publishing.

I have no gray hair, but I have perenially sore feet and legs from the pounding I've given them. From the waist down, I feel 50 years old on good days, 70 or 80 on bad ones. From

How old would you be? Two of the world's great runners side by side, each, having set several world records in recent years, is at a peak in his career. Duncan McClean is 94; John Walker is 23. Who can predict what further great accomplishments lie in store for these two?

the waist up, I look ten years younger than my real age (unless you look closely). The hair, the clothes, the weight all are pretty much as they were when I left school.

In many ways, I have more of a teenager's outlook now than I did when I was in my teens. I wouldn't let myself be young then. I was too busy trying to grow up fast and acting twice my age. Now, I act half my age. I'm the kid I wouldn't let myself be before.

The calendar puts me at 35. Technically, this disqualifies me from a book titled *Running after Forty*. But I write now because everyone my age is moving in that direction, and 35 is in some ways a more important landmark on that journey than 40 is.

Thirty-five is the halfway mark. Since the life expectancy of Americans is about 70, 35 is the end of growing up and the start of growing old. When we get to the top of this hill, we see for the first time where we're headed—and know we don't want to go.

Gail Sheehy calls the 35th birthday, or thereabouts, one of the "predictable crises of adult life." She must be right, because her book *Passages* has struck enough nerves to become a best-seller.

At 35, the dreams haven't come true and look like they never will. The world is seen through glasses, and not rose-colored ones. The lines around the mouth and eyes are deepening, and the skin at the jowls is sagging even on those of us who've stayed lean. The hairline is retreating. We can't stay up past midnight any more and expect to greet the dawn with a smile on our lips and a song in our hearts the next morning. We have responsibilities, obligations, worries that cause us to walk heavily and wearily.

It is not coincidence that so many people take up running in their mid-30s, or start to train and compete more seriously at that age. It's a way, first, to resist aging, then later to make peace with that process.

Thirty-five not only starts the "second half." It begins a new life cycle. Author Sheehy says we make fresh starts about every seven years, and that these major changes in direction don't come smoothly. My pattern is typical.

The first cycle started, of course, with the biggest event of all—being born. I spent my first seven years as an apprentice person, learning more information and skills then than I'd pick up the rest of the years combined.

At seven, two big things happened. I learned to read and write well enough to communicate and be communicated to that way. And I began to play at sports in an organized way.

I found my best sport at 14. That's when I became a runner, a serious runner who stayed that way for seven years. I raced and trained so hard that I couldn't last at that intensity.

At 21, I became an apprentice writer and editor. I decided this was what I wanted to do with my working life. Meanwhile, my running took a sudden turn for the slower and easier at that age.

Two things happened at 28. I got married, and I got more serious about writing. This cycle would yield two children and three published books (plus three more as-yet-unpublished ones).

By 35, I'd succeeded so well in my job that I couldn't do my work any more. I spent all day meeting with, writing letters to and calling other writers. So I quit my job at its apparent peak and moved to the country to write fulltime.

Each change sounds so natural, so right as I look back quickly. What this summary doesn't show is the months of doubt and fear surrounding the major turns of a lifetime. The negatives show up first, to be blotted out later by positives.

As the second half and the new seven-year cycle move on, I begin to see the plus side of getting older:

- The pride of still running well even though I have more than a few years on me.
- The wisdom that only comes with experience, and the experience to use wisely what I know.
- The hardness that comes with absorbing 35 years of knocks, and the softness that comes with adjusting to change instead of fighting it.
- The patience to let things happen at their own pace.
- The assurance to go my own way, in my own way, at my own rate, without worrying about how other people do things.

Age is what we make it—a feeling that we're fulfilling our

allotted quota of years or emptying it with age. Renee Taylor writes about some of the longest-living people on earth, the Hunza of Pakistan, who take the first approach.

In Hunza, Taylor says, "Time is not measured by clocks or calendars. Time is judged by the changing of the seasons, and each season brings a feeling of newness, not a fear that time is slipping irrevocably away."

Taylor quotes the Mir (king) of Hunza as saying a person's life divides into three periods: "The young years, the middle years, and the *rich* years. In the young years, there is pleasure and excitement and the yearning for knowledge. In the middle years, there is development of poise and appreciation, along with the pleasures, the excitement, and the yearnings of the young years. In the rich years—by far the best period of all—there is mellowness, understanding, the ability to judge, and the great gift of tolerance—all of this combined with the qualities of the two previous periods.

"The keynote of life is growth, not aging. Life does not grow old. The life that flows through us at 80 is the same that energized us in infancy. It does not grow old or weak. So-called age is the deterioration of enthusiasm, faith to live, and will to progress."

How old would you be if you didn't know your age?

Part One

Masters Running

Chapter 1

Getting Fit

Imagine yourself in the following situations:

1. Your daughter, on a weekend home from college, challenges you to one of those rousing tennis games you enjoyed so much five years ago.

2. Returning to a client's office after lunch you find the elevator is out and you must climb four flights of stairs if you are to close the deal you have been negotiating.

3. You are involved in a serious accident on a country road—a half-mile run to the nearest house becomes a matter of life and death for an injured friend.

Can you still hold your own against your daughter or do you beg off? Do you close the deal on the stairway or huff and puff in your client's office for several minutes before being able to speak? Does it take you four minutes to get help for your friend or fifteen?

Pardon the melodrama, but if you are representative of Americans over 40, you probably feel a sense of unease at the prospect of scenes like those above. You are very probably in better shape than most people your age, however. In epidemic proportions, people in their forties and fifties are finding even office routine—typing, answering the telephone, walking the hallways—fatiguing, fatiguing in the same way you might find tackling four flights of stairs fatiguing.

We can assume you are in better shape because people in such poor shape are not likely to be interested in browsing through a bookstore—too demanding. Even if they did and were interested in improving their condition as well, they'd probably come away with a book titled something like *Total Fitness without Lifting a Finger.* The idea of tackling something as strenuous as running is as alien as the idea of living without television.

You, like most people over 40 who take up running, very probably are more active than average now or were more active than average in your twenties. You probably participated in athletics in high school or college. No matter; the fact that you are reading a book on running is evidence of your intentions. Whether you are considering running for the first time or have already tried it, we hope this book will show you the way to an exhilarating experience in sport fitness.

FITNESS

Let's hope you don't need a chapter on the fitness benefits running can provide to convince you to take up running. Those who have started running because of concern over health usually find such concerns pale after a few months; they become hooked on other aspects. Still, it would be nice to know what you may get from a regular program of running.

What you will get from running is fit. If you exercise at 70 to 85 percent of your maximum heart rate (see chapter 8) for twenty minutes at a time every other day, you will get fit and continue to get fitter as the months go by. You will get almost as fit as someone who exceeds the above formula by a factor of two, three, even four. To try to explain what "fitness" is, we will break it down into six component areas: health fitness, aerobic fitness, organ fitness, mental fitness, body fat, and flexibility.

Health Fitness

Concern for the well-being of the heart increases dramatically as one approaches 40. Many people have been attracted to running by claims that "the marathon lifestyle provides immunity to myocardial infarction." Such pronouncements simply muddy the waters.

Running is a cure for only one disease—Habitual Inactivity. Particularly if accompanied by concern for diet and rest, a ban on smoking and drugs, and moderation in alcohol consumption, running can be a 100 percent cure for Habitual Inactivity. And, to the extent that Habitual Inactivity is linked to heart attack, asthma, hypertension, gout, ulcers, arthritis, senility, backache, constipation, insomnia, headache, allergies, and a host of other complaints, running may also reduce their incidence.

Aerobic Fitness

The principal measure of fitness is maximum oxygen uptake, usually expressed as the number of millimeters of oxygen consumed per kilogram of body mass per minute at maximum exertions (chapter 8 also contains a discussion). This measure indicates how much oxygen the body can process for turning sugars and fats into energy. Aerobic capacity has seven components:

1. Vital Capacity—the volume of air the lungs will hold.
2. Breathing Capacity—the rate at which the lungs can be emptied and refilled.
3. Pulmonary Ventilation and Diffusion—the ability of the blood to extract oxygen from the lungs.
4. Oxygen Capacity of the Blood—the amount of oxygen the blood can carry.
5. Cardiac Output—the ability of the heart to circulate the blood.
6. Capillarization—the extent to which capillaries (the blood vessels in which oxygen transfer takes place) permeate the tissues.
7. Utilization—the efficiency of the tissues at combusting glycogen and fats.

Among the ways aerobic exercise (exercise paced so that oxygen intake accounts for nearly all of the energy expended as opposed to anaerobic exercise—that which proceeds faster than the body can provide oxygen for efficient energy production) improves maximum oxygen uptake are

1. increasing the size and elasticity of the lungs
2. strengthening the diaphragm, intercostals, and other muscles of breathing
3. increasing the volume of blood in the body and the amount of hemoglobin in the blood
4. adding literally miles of capillaries to the circulatory system
5. increasing the size and strength of the heart
6. increasing the number, size, and enzyme content of the mitochondria, the cells within the muscles where fuel is burned.

Of all athletes, distance runners have the highest maximum oxygen capacity. It follows that running is the best means for improving aerobic fitness.

Organ Fitness

Many organs and functions of the body other than the heart and lungs benefit from running. The body's largest organ, the skin, becomes much more efficient at heat dissipation. Runners report improved bowel regularity and digestive ability. Kidneys and bladder function better. The endocrine system keeps a better hormone balance. Bones get stronger, and decalcification is reversed among older runners. Most runners report improved sexual functioning. Even the senses, especially taste and smell, get a boost.

Mental Fitness

The most frequently mentioned benefit of running is "it relaxes me." One study showed that seventeen minutes of running produced changes in the body similar to a normal dose of valium. Runners also report enhanced alertness, sounder sleep, a greater sense of well-being, higher self-esteem, improved creativity, and being more in tune with people and events.

Running improves ability to handle stress. Runners often get better attuned to their pain threshholds and other body signals. Running has been used with some success in the treatment of schizophrenia.

Body Fat

In one way of looking at it, excess body fat is a boon—the more extra weight you carry, the more work you accomplish with each step. The realistic way to look at it, however, is that excess body fat represents a mass of tissue which requires maintenance by the body while providing no benefits, only several detriments.

Even the scrawniest of runners, one with only 5 percent body fat has a virtually limitless supply of fat fuel, so you see that even the normal range of about 15 percent body fat is a luxury. The body prefers to burn sugars for its energy and only burns fat as a back-up fuel. To make the body an efficient fat burner, you will need to include runs of longer than forty-five minutes in your regimen weekly or more often.

One excess pound of weight will cost about one minute of lost time over the course of a marathon; twenty pounds will cost about seventeen minutes. Each mile run, whether fast or slow, burns about one hundred calories. It takes 3,500 calories to get rid of one pound of fat. It's not difficult to eat 3,500 calories in one sitting, but it can be excruciating to run thirty-five miles a day. If you want to lose weight, you will need to watch your calorie intake (don't go on a crash diet while undertaking a running program, however—you can overstress your body).

Any adult who takes up strenuous exercise is likely to be bombarded with suggestions for special diets. Be especially skeptical of high-protein diets, which can produce ammonia and other wastes in your system during exercise. The best advice is to eat mostly raw fruits and vegetables; drink water, beer, and juices; eat meats and dairy products in moderation; and avoid all greasy or sugary foods. The second best advice is to stick with your present eating habits, attempting any special diet only after you've had time to get comfortable with your exercise program.

Flexibility

Flexibility is the range of movement in joints and tissues. You can have too much flexibility, but it is much more likely that you have too little. Habitual Inactivity is a greater limiter of flexibility; joints stiffen, collagen plugs the tissues, joint surfaces dry out, nerves dull, pain creeps into movement.

While running will wash your body with refreshing fluids and bring some of the spring back to your motion, it ultimately is an enemy of flexibility. The muscular contractions of running cause the muscles to tighten. Stretching is the antidote, and that is discussed in chapter 9.

MEDICAL SCREENING

You probably know right now whether you intend to see a doctor or not in connection with your running program. If you do, unless you have a high-risk profile (heavy smoker/drinker, obese, history of heart problems, etcetera) make the appointment and go ahead with your workouts. You run very little risk of ill effects, and you'll be able to ask much more informative questions when you do see your physician.

Also, if you intend to see a doctor, realize that five out of six physicians are no more informed than you are about the effects of exercise. The irresponsibility of the medical profession in this regard is scandalous, but the situation is changing. You will save yourself much trouble if you will inquire at a running club for the names of member physicians.

If you do not care to see a physician, you are in good company. Most people don't bother, and most runners queried in the course of this book (see chapter 3) did not recommend seeing a physician. Even physicians themselves are divided on the value and accuracy of pre-exercise screening. For your information, a serious cardiac incident is precipitated once every 15,000 stress tests. Since the stress tests are taken at maximal level and you will be working out one-fourth below that, your chances of never having any serious incident are excellent.

Podiatrists

The most commonly needed medical assistance for runners is for leg and foot problems. Podiatrists have come to be known as the runner's doctor. Given the incredibly high occurrence of posture and gait problems, it's no wonder that two out of five

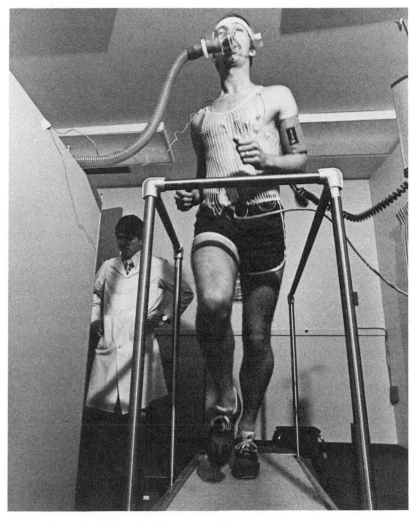

A treadmill test for aerobic capacity

runners consult a podiatrist. You may want to schedule a visit to a podiatrist a couple of months down the road anyway, particularly if you know you have postural or mechanical defects or if you experience pains from running.

Always take your running shoes with you to your podiatrist so he or she can examine them for unusual wear. And again, save yourself some trouble by locating a podiatrist who also runs.

BEGINNING

The beginning is both the best and the worst phase of a running program. Best because improvements are more noticeable, worst because there is so much to assimilate and adjust to all at once.

Chapters 7 and 8 will give more advice on structuring your program, but the basic advice is this:

- Don't try to do too much at once. Don't start dieting, meditating, running, yoga all at the same time—each takes full concentration in the beginning.
- Don't overdo it and don't underdo it. Don't wear yourself out, but don't fail to get the aerobic conditioning you need.
- Cut back on smoking and food consumption. Alcohol intake of up to two ounces a day may be good for you, but don't drink to excess.
- Get plenty of rest and sleep.
- *Do not run without wearing top-quality running shoes.*

That should do it. Happy running!

Chapter 2

Masters Track
Truman Clark

"He said he wasn't going to have any masters events in meets he directed again, because he was afraid someone would topple over from a heart attack. His wife suggested that *he* was more likely to have one than any of the master runners."

A runner who participated in the "masters mile" in a large track meet about a decade ago remembers this reaction to the idea of people over the age of 40 running competitively. True to his word, that meet director, a former All-American football player, has avoided masters events in subsequent track meets under his direction. But in spite of this man and a few others like him, masters track has grown in both numbers and importance. Today it is perhaps the most innovative and interesting segment of the sport.

The Need for Masters Track

Masters track, just as has been the case with other portions of "age-group" track in the United States, has been a response to wide-spread needs and interests that were not being met. Before the advent of masters track, the runner who competed in college found his (and it usually was only men) opportunities for competing decreasing in direct correlation with his age: the further he got from college age, the less likely he could find track meets that were available to an "old man" like himself. If he was a distance runner, he was lucky, for road-running was

11

a possibility in at least some areas of the country. But a sprinter, hurdler, or middle distance runner had at best the prospect of track "seasons" consisting only of a few summer all-comers meets (if there were any in his area), in which he could compete with the "college boys" at an increasing disadvantage. And for the person who had never been a competitive runner in high school or college, or for the runner well over 40, being tossed into a race with athletes who were entering the all-comers meets after college track seasons, was obviously intimidating.

The first tentative step toward supplying this need for competitive track opportunities came in the mid-1960s with the addition of a "masters mile" to some summer all-comers meets and even some large indoor and outdoor meets in which world-class younger runners were the open runners. There were mixed motives in presenting these "masters miles," such as a desire to make use of a runner who had been competitive as an open runner well into his thirties, and who was well-known to track fans of the area.

Such races were, however, rarely found other than on the west and east coasts, they were only for men, and they obviously offered nothing for the over-40 athlete who wasn't a miler. And sometimes those "masters miles" were not interjected among the other events of a meet, but rather scheduled either for the very first or the very end of a meet, so that the masters ran in front of only a fraction of the spectators who attended the meet. (Many of these problems remain today in some large open meets that include masters events.)

It was during that same decade that complete track meets for masters began to appear. In part, this was the result of the formation of running clubs that were basically masters, and masters segments of existing track clubs growing large enough to have their own meets. And it was also partly the work of some masters athletes in the San Diego area.

Masters Track and Field Championship

David Pain and Augie Escamilla were responsible for helping persuade a number of track meet directors to add events for masters to their meets. Along with Ken Bernard and the

Masters track

backing of the large and active San Diego Track Club, they organized in 1968 a hopefully-named First Annual U.S. Masters Track and Field Championship. There were mostly athletes from Southern California at that first championship, but also a scattering of competitors from at least ten other states and Canada. This meet was the breakthrough for masters track, and David Pain has been called by some knowledgeable people "the father of masters track." At that first meet were several runners (and field event performers) who had been well-known younger runners, including George Rhoden, who won two gold medals in the 1952 Olympic Games, and John Kelley of Boston Marathon fame.

The U.S. Masters Track and Field Championships continued to be held in San Diego under the direction of Pain, Bernard, Escamilla and others through 1973. During that time a number of changes occurred. Probably the most important of these was the meet's identification with the A.A.U. The Amateur Athletic Union of the United States was becoming increasingly aware of the needs and interests of masters, and for a couple of years A.A.U. officials discussed with Pain the possibility of his San Diego championship meet being made an official national A.A.U. championship. Pain says, "I was hesitant," because of the A.A.U. rules about coaches, trainers, and people who had competed professionally in other sports—none were then eligible to compete in A.A.U. meets of any sort. Gradually, the A.A.U. accepted the position that in masters track, such "professionalism" would not bar a person from competition. The program for the 1971 San Diego meet identified it both with its previous title, but also as the First Annual A.A.U. Masters Track and Field Championship.

Another drawback to A.A.U. acceptance of masters track was thinking similar to that of the All-American football player mentioned earlier. A man who was in those years closely involved both with masters track and the A.A.U. has said that "some mossbacks" then in A.A.U. posts "didn't want to stamp 'AAU' on the masters program, because they were afraid of a *death*." These officials held out some time for all masters athletes having to undergo an electrocardiogram test before being allowed to compete. One man largely responsible for convincing these officials that such a course wasn't necessary was Bob Giegengack, long the track coach at Yale.

In addition to its merger with the A.A.U., the national masters meet saw some other changes before it left San Diego. Through the first three years all the events were in yards and miles, but in 1971 the three- and six-mile runs were made 5,000 and 10,000 meter events, and a 3,000 meter steeplechase was added. In 1971 there was a "Special Women's Mile," and women's events were added to the meet schedule on a rather haphazard basis, with a 400 meters, a 1,500 meters, and a 5,000 meters in the 1972 meet, only 200, 1,500, and five-kilometer races in 1973, and since then a continuation of isolated events and sparse numbers of women competitors. In the 1978 national championship meet, women were in every event (including the high hurdles and 400 meter hurdles) except the steeplechase.

In addition to some Canadians, this national masters championship has since 1973 usually attracted some foreign athletes.

The big year for this was 1975, because the meet was held in White Plains, New York, within a week of the big international masters championships in Toronto, so that a number of individuals competed in both meets.

Since 1973 this meet has been known only as the "A.A.U. Masters National Track and Field Championship," and it has been held twice in Gresham, Oregon (where it will take place again in 1979), as well as White Plains, Chicago, and Atlanta. And other large-scale competitions for masters are appearing. During the last few years there has also been a national indoor masters track championship. The 1979 indoor meet was in Ann Arbor, Michigan, and had entrants from almost half the states as well as Canada. In addition, there are now each year seven outdoor regional A.A.U. track championships for masters, three indoor regional meets, and numerous district championships. Many clubs, such as the Corona Del Mar Track Club and the Southern California Striders, now put on their own masters relay meets.

World Championships

Masters track has definitely become international. Again, David Pain of San Diego played an important role, making contacts in Europe, leading to an "International Veterans Athletic Meeting" in 1972 in London. That meet, with competitors from the United States, Australia, Ireland, the Netherlands, Israel, Canada, and the host Great Britain, was a forerunner of the World Masters Track and Field Championships held every two years since 1975. The first of these meets was in Toronto, Canada, and had 1,400 competitors. The 1977 meet was in Gothenburg, Sweden, and totaled more than two thousand athletes—almost certainly the largest single track meet ever held. Internationally, over-40 runners are often called "veterans" rather than "masters." And outside the United States women "masters" usually begin at age 35 rather than 40. Hanover, Germany, was the site of the World Masters meet in August, 1979. European masters held thier first championship track meet in Italy in 1978. Just as in the United States, there are increasing numbers of runners coming into European masters track who were once Olympians—even world record holders. Dave Power and Al Thomas of Australia, Michel Bernard of France, and Gaston Roelants of Belgium are some of the more famous world-class runners who have now lent their names to the masters movement.

The Growth of Masters Track

One reason why masters track has burgeoned is the entry policy of their meets: anyone can enter (assuming the person is the correct age), and enter *any* events—even something one hasn't tried before. Thus, any masters runner who can get to a meet can compete in it, without having to achieve some qualifying standard. Perhaps a few of the athletes who were "bigname" in their younger days may eventually object to this open-entry policy, but so far everyone has been pleased with it.

Those runners with national and world-class backgrounds have among them now some individuals of "the embarrassed school," as one master describes them. These are athletes who feel self-conscious about competing against "old guys," rather than world-class younger runners. Most masters who competed even reasonably successfully before turning 40 can remember going through one small phase of this. That was when they were in their 30s, sitting at a track meet watching some men over 40 run, thinking, "How slow! Could I ever run off from them, if I were 40!" Most masters quickly get over any oddness they feel about entering age-group competition, even though at first they may mentally echo the words of one well-known distance runner on the eve of his first masters race: "I've never been this old before!"

Masters are now a large and important part of A.A.U. track, with more than two thousand masters registered in track and field (many others who take part in track meets are distance runners registered with the A.A.U. only in long-distance running). The masters has its own committee in the A.A.U. track and field structure. The co-chairman of that masters committee, Bob Fine of New York, proudly tells how healthy masters track is: "The masters are self-sufficient. We're the only committee that has never asked for any of the money from the national championships."

One sign that masters track is perhaps on the verge of an even greater leap forward, may be the sizeable contingent of athletes now competing as "sub-masters." These track men and women, 35 to 39 years old, were the largest group in attendance at the 1979 indoor A.A.U. masters track championship. This group has long been held in a sort of limbo between open competition and masters track. From the early years of masters outdoor championships in San Diego, women in this age group (and even younger) were provided some special opportunities to run more or less like exhibition races. And at least by 1976 there were sub-masters events for men along with the regular masters divisions at the national meet. Technically, the sub-masters (in the fall of 1978 the A.A.U. decided to label them "age-groupers") are not under the masters committee, and register with the A.A.U. as open athletes. But as a practical matter, and a friendly action, they are now included in the masters meets, nationally and locally.

The status of women in masters track has also been a question. Although they now are included in the national masters championships, as well as most regional and district meets, they are still registered solely under the jurisdiction of the A.A.U.'s womens track and field committee, rather than being a part of the oversight of the masters committee or having their own women's masters committee. One problem has been that there are not nearly the numbers of women over 40 in track and field that there are in long-distance running (in which they are combined with the men in one A.A.U. committtee). In many events at the Atlanta national masters meet in 1978, there were only one or two women per age division.

Senior Olympics

So far in this discussion of masters track, we have dealt entirely with A.A.U. programs. But there is another organization which has been involved with masters track and field in the United States. Senior Olympics International is an unusual organization, the product of an unusual man, Warren Blaney.

In 1970 Blaney put together his first Senior Olympics competitions—in swimming, track and field, and the marathon. Even though his advertising for the events was then largely confined to "word of mouth," a total of about 175 people entered the

At the starting line of the Examiner Games

three sports. Since that time, Blaney's operation has grown to become a full-time occupation for himself and his son, Worth Blaney. They administer and advertise a widespread schedule of seventeen "sports" (they have recently added harmonica playing and everything from Frisbee to shuffleboard competition) from a tiny office on Wilshire Boulevard in Los Angeles. Much of the office consists of file cabinets with the names and addresses of thousands of people who have expressed an interest in, or participated in, the Senior Olympics. The track and field portion of the Senior Olympics has now grown to about 500 entrants in 1978. Senior Olympics meets have always been held on good tracks in the Los Angeles area—the Coliseum in 1970 and 1971, California State University at Los Angeles in 1972, UCLA in 1973, University of California at Irvine 1974 through 1978, and this year the brand-new track at the University of Southern California.

Blaney and Senior Olympics are controversial. He is described by some people as everything from "a man who pretends very hard to be senile," to "a rip-off artist." Critics point to the high entry fees for the Senior Olympics ($7 for the first event, $3 for each additional one), and the way people are charged for everything else from copies of the results to Senior Olympics patches. They point out that his organization is quite casual about everything from making a schedule clear as to when an event will be run to the accuracy of marks. Blaney admits that such details are not terribly important to him; the Senior Olympics has no interest in ever purchasing electronic timing equipment, wind gauges, or even stop watches ("A lot of runners bring their own," says Blaney). The Senior Olympics organization (the two Blaneys) does not actually run the track meet, but relies upon local volunteers, as it does in every sport. And one has only to listen to Blaney for a few minutes to realize that this non-profit organization is, after all, a business with a fairly low overhead.

Warren Blaney ignores all this, as he energetically dashes off piles of work while talking at machine-gun pace. His speech is littered with the cliches and aphorisms that abound in the printed Senior Olympics literature: "Family fun! Positive action, positive thought, creating a new adult image! The family that plays together, stays together! We want to help people help themselves!" He proudly asserts that the Senior Olympics helped to prod the A.A.U. into meeting the needs of people who are beyond college age. His organization, says Blaney, preceded the A.A.U. in using five-year age divisions, giving women equal status and competitive opportunities, allowing people who were technically "professionals" to participate, and generally in making track and field for older athletes a counterpart to the international competition available to younger athletes. In all this, he is largely correct; the Senior Olympics *did* emphasize each of those things a bit earlier than the A.A.U.

Blaney says that the Senior Olympics originally tried to work hand-in-hand with the A.A.U., "not for money but together as helpers," and that he still holds out a welcome mat toward cooperation with the A.A.U., but that it has been "not very friendly." This is a bit of understatement, both by Blaney's own account, and that of people who think of him somewhat as a kook and con man but who nevertheless see the A.A.U. as unnecessarily hostile to the Senior Olympics. The A.A.U., says Blaney, has threatened sanctions against athletes who compete in the Senior Olympics, and one A.A.U. official long ago boasted to Blaney that, "I'll give you a year-and-a-half" before the A.A.U. would bury the Senior Olympics. (There is, however, nothing presently noticeable in the way of a belligerent stance by the A.A.U. toward the Senior Olympics; it would seem that at this time that A.A.U.'s position is to *ignore* the Senior Olympics.) Actually, many runners who are regulars in A.A.U.-certified events also compete in the Senior Olympics. Perhaps because they are mostly masters and other athletes who are far from "national class," no one makes a fuss about it. And Blaney proudly notes that "we have some friends in the A.A.U.," some of whom serve as timers and judges at the Senior Olympics track meets each year.

Even with its problems and separateness from the rest of American masters track, the Senior Olympics does bring track into the lives of many people. A typical statement is that of Shirley Kinsey of Southern California, now a leader in A.A.U. women's age-group track, who traces her own athletic career to the Senior Olympics: "It was the only thing that was around."

Masters Records

Although the Senior Olympics is unconcerned about the verification of track and field marks, masters as a whole are interested in accurate timing, as well as the collection of records in different events. Until 1972 the A.A.U. also expressed no concern over masters marks, and it still does not actually *keep* masters records. The one name associated with every detail of track and field record-keeping for competitors beyond college age, is Pete Mundle (see appendix).

Mundle is perfectly suited to this role of record-keeper for masters track. As an undergraduate at the University of Oregon, later as a runner in open track well into his late thirties, then as one of the first participants in "masters miles," and since then a premier figure in masters distance running to his present age 51, Pete has been associated often with *setting* records. At any given time, he may hold as many as a dozen or more national

Peter Mundle leading

or world records for his current age, or some of his earlier ages, at distances from a mile through a marathon. And he is a mathematician by profession, with studies at Oregon (M.S.) and the University of London. Part of his interest in running has been his interest in track statistics: "I've been doing that all my life." When someone wants to know what the U.S. best is for a 41-year-old man at 40 miles on a track, or for a 52-year-old woman at one-hour on the track, they come to Mundle: somewhere in his mass of statistics, he has a computer print-out with that precise information. Katherine Brieger of Berkeley is now amassing women's records in the same way, and together with Jack Shepard of Westminster, California, they are the collectors and disseminators of records for all age-group track in the United States.

Ted Vogel nips Jim Hartshorne at the finish line

Pete (and Brieger) gets some track results directly from meet directors, others from *Track and Field News* (through which he has an age-group record book published), and still more results by personally attending many masters meets, even when he is injured and cannot compete. The A.A.U. is pleased to work with Pete, and he is its "records chairman" for masters track. A.A.U. officials know the precise high standards of Pete's work with records—when he confirms that someone set a record, it was set; there is no effort by the A.A.U. or anyone else to further verify a mark. Bob Fine, masters co-chairman, happily notes that the A.A.U. plans to use Mundle's information in publishing (annually, or more often) lists of masters' marks, and from that, awarding yearly "All-American" awards.

Amateur Standing

Until last year, masters track wrestled with the problem of amateur standing. Initially, the A.A.U. held to its position that coaches, trainers, and people who had been professionals in other sports, were ineligible for masters track. Thanks to people like David Pain, Ken Bernard, Bob Fine, and others, the A.A.U. began as early as 1971 to modify its stand on this sticky point, but the International Amateur Athletic Federation (I.A.A.F.) was, in Pain's words, "absolutely uncompromising." Finally, in 1978, the I.A.A.F. decided it can survive while ignoring for masters its official stance regarding "professionalism."

The lengthy debate, and some other issues, contributed to David Pain dropping his work with the U.S. masters program a few years ago, because he felt that some A.A.U. and I.A.A.F. officials "wanted to build up their own positions" and forced him to "get involved with politics, which depressed me, because I thought masters' track should be *beyond* politics." For all that he is obviously proud of the many things he accomplished in the decade of his involvement with masters track, and in spite of his affirmation that he has some good friends in the A.A.U., it is obvious that Pain was frustrated by those past track wars.

Bob Fine disagrees with the viewpoint taken by Pain and some others who have broken with the A.A.U. Fine argues that, "We are the *only* committee in the A.A.U. that opens up our yearly meeting to *anyone*, and we open it up completely, to all the masters athletes who want to come. Anyone can help make the rules. The *athletes* run our committee, so when a master complains about something, he's really complaining about what his fellow runners have done." He pleads with dissident masters athletes to get involved, take positions on local committees of the A.A.U. and attend these annual meetings.

A minor problem in masters track is mentioned by Fine: "There's a split between long distance and track and field, which I find disturbing." Often, such a gulf will be felt even within a single masters track club.

People associated with masters track are more prone to discuss its contributions and prospects for the future, than problems. Veteran track runner and writer Tom Sturak sees two major contributions to track as a whole that have been made by masters track. First, the recent modification of A.A.U. and I.A.A.F. positions toward professionalism and masters shows that "masters have helped the world athletic bodies loosen up, and to take a closer, more realistic, look at this issue." Second, the very success of the masters in holding international track meets far larger than the Olympic Games is a good argument in favor of adding distance races for women to the Olympics. If the masters can efficiently handle two thousand or more entrants in their championships, certainly the Olympics, with its far larger budget, can manage to expand the number of athletes in it by a couple of hundred women in five- and ten-kilometer races and a marathon.

Several new things are on the verge of being added to masters track. The Occidental Life Insurance Company will shortly begin publication of a monthly newsletter. The A.A.U., as already mentioned, plans to start awarding "All-American" honors to the top five masters in each track event every year. And Bob Fine hopes that the A.A.U. will also begin to publish a national masters directory, which will help to inform people better. No one can deny that U.S. masters track seems to be just now getting into full stride.

Truman Clark, holder of five age-group records, is a professor of Political Science at Pepperdine University in Malibu, California. This chapter appeared previously in Runner's World.

Chapter 3

Motivation

The unmotivated don't run. Something has to stir the soul before the legs will start to churn. Since we seldom anymore run after food or to avoid becoming food, we turn elsewhere for our motivation.

Why do people run these days? That will be discussed in this chapter based on responses masters runners gave to a survey conducted for this book. But motivation is a more complex subject than just "why run." Why run a particular distance, a 10 K for instance, or a marathon, or an ultramarathon? Why race? Can you be too motivated? First, the simple side of the subject.

WHY RUN

Running is a social phenomenon. There was a time when a chapter like this one in a running book would concern itself with the image and acceptability of running. Many people, older people in particular, had to be convinced that running was something that was all right to do. Jim Fixx included an amusing anecdote in *The Complete Book of Running* about the deception necessary to keep coworkers from learning about his lunchtime runs. But there are no more closet joggers, not at a time when Frank Shorter and Jim Fixx grace our television commercials and the President and members of

Congress can be seen burning up the streets of Washington, D.C. (see Profiles).

However, the acceptability of running merely allows people to run without feeling too self-conscious. Except for those who run solely at the urging of spouse or friends, social reasons don't make anyone run.

In the survey conducted for this book, some one hundred masters runners were contacted. Nearly all returned the questionnaire. One thing that became obvious quickly is that it was much easier to pinpoint why someone kept running than why he or she started running.

Most people harbor thoughts about their health and appearance, and, thanks largely to Dr. Kenneth Cooper's books, most people realize that vigorous exercise is required to maintain health and appearance. But a spark is needed to ignite all of this thought into action. For many the spark is embarrassment—when playing with the kids or walking a flight of stairs they discover they don't have the wind they thought they did, or one morning they tip the scales at an alarming weight. For some, unfortunately, a heart attack has supplied the incentive. Others have been inspired by seeing a Marcie Trent or a Ruth Anderson and thinking "if she can do it, so can I."

In addition to whatever spark that actually got them running, most people can point to a lot of other background reasons: a magazine article or book read, friends who run, a "Y" or track nearby, or a doctor's admonition about high blood pressure or high cholesterol levels. In short, few can name one clear-cut circumstance that got them started running. However, all runners seem to know exactly why they keep running. Though running offers numerous benefits, runners can go into extensive detail on the ones that are important to them. Here are the ones that we received on the survey, ranked according to the number of positive responses.

1. Running relaxes me. It clears my mind.   89
2. I have more stamina. I feel stronger.   84
3. I get a sense of accomplishment. My self-esteem is
   enhanced.   76
4. I feel more vigorous and alert.   72
5. I get a great sense of enjoyment out of running. It's fun.   72

6. I feel like doing more work. I get more done.   64

7. I worry less about my heart and my health.   55

8. Running has beneficial effects on my sleeping, breathing, and diet.   49

9. I excel at running. I enjoy getting complimented on my ability.   44

10. My weight, posture, and general appearance have all been improved.   34

(Scores are based on total response versus the potential strongly positive response. The scale ranges from 100 to -100, so that 34, for instance, still represents a pretty strong consensus.)

FOR BEGINNERS

Ask veteran runners why they run and they will usually mention several of the benefits listed above. Ask veteran runners why they run on any given day and you'll find yourself in fuzzy territory. Usual responses include: "I don't feel good unless I run" or "It's just part of my routine."

For the beginner, getting to the point at which running is "just part of your routine" is pretty much the whole challenge. Beginning runners often find it a battle just to reach into the closet for those running shoes. And don't expect much help from experienced runners; unless they've had a recent comeback after a layoff to remind them, they've long since forgotten what you're going through.

Daily Routine

Nobody quits running. Nobody declares, "Well, this isn't what I thought it would be. I'm not going to do it any more." Typically, a one-day layoff turns into two, then into three, and so on until the accumulated benefits are lost and running again means starting over from scratch.

The perfect way to insure you do not fall into this all-too-common syndrome is to make your workout a daily routine, regardless of what comes up. This does not mean you have to run every day. It means you suit up every day, go somewhere to run, and do your stretches. Run if you feel like it. If you don't feel like running, walk around until you do. If after walking you still don't feel like running, stretch out on the grass and relax. Relaxing the muscles today will mean you get more benefit from yesterday's run anyway—the one that has you so tired to begin with.

Even if you get home at midnight with an early day ahead of you, if you haven't run, change into your running togs, go out in the yard, stretch, walk a block, and only then retire. Your body—whatever mechanism in it that rebels against establishing new routines—quickly gives up its intention of sapping your will in the face of such dedication.

If you must take a regular day off, Tuesdays for instance, Wednesday becomes critical. No matter what, don't miss Wednesday's workout.

While sticking to a daily routine is the sure-fire way to maintain a running program, there are some other helpful gimmicks.

Classes and Clubs

Fortunate are those with exercise facilities at their place of work. Throw in a fitness program and coworkers who are enthusiastic about it and you're home free.

The next best thing is a convenient class or club. YMCAs offer some excellent classes. Additional advantages of such classes usually include medical screening, a structured program, individual coaching, immediate feedback on your technique, and meeting people.

Many running clubs offer facilities and instruction. Others may be nothing more than a weekly get-together. You should get in the habit of going to those weekly functions so that even if you let yourself down and skip a whole week, the commitment to that club meeting will get you going again before it's too late.

Diaries

Keeping a daily log of their running activity is a great source of motivation for many. About one-third of the respondents to our survey thought diaries were essential; another third had no opinion on the matter; and the last third thought they were a device of the devil to take the joy out of running.

Some find it takes more discipline to keep a diary than to run. Others need written evidence to keep them honest about their running. Keeping a diary is such a personality thing that you probably already know whether you'll do it or not.

If you do keep one, you will find it a great source of information for setting goals, avoiding injury, and determining peak performance periods. A sample diary is reproduced in this chapter.

Adventure Running

Some runners keep going by making a list of places they want to see on the run. The places to run to may be near home, or the runner may prefer to travel to various parks, campuses, woodland trails, or whatever. Running to new places each day keeps the runner's outlook fresh and makes it easier to get out there each day. You'll get a big boost from passing stores and other spots on foot that you would only have gone to by car weeks earlier.

On the other hand, there are those runners who prefer the same track or trail every time. The incentive to better their performance on a standard course is the motivation they need.

If there is a running guide to your city, you might set your sights on running every path listed. That is the stamp-album approach. After a while, the quest to complete the collection can be strong motivation indeed. Beware the letdown once you've accomplished your mission. Such letdowns have occurred with runners who have achieved long-sought goals, such as a sub-3:00 marathon.

Another gimmick of this sort is to keep a map. Start with a map of your city. Each day draw a line representing the distance you covered. Soon you will have a line across the city. Progress to a county map, state map, United States map, and finally a globe. Unless you live in Rhode Island, you should be hooked on running long before you cross the state map.

WEEK OF __January 7-13__

GOALS FOR WEEK __Start 8-week__
__buildup for marathon March - 50 miles__

No one talks or writes so enthusiastically as when he is telling someone else
what is bad for him. But convincing him of the errors of his ways is only
half the job. The other half is outlining a corrective program.

SUNDAY __7th__

Tired from yesterday's long run.

PACE __8:18__ WEATHER __32° Clear__ DISTANCE __5__ WEEK TOTAL __5__

MONDAY __8th__

Still low on energy

PACE __7:57__ WEATHER __35° Clear__ DISTANCE __6__ WEEK TOTAL __11__

TUESDAY __9th__

Sub-8:00 despite snow!!

PACE __7:50__ WEATHER __30° Snow__ DISTANCE __8__ WEEK TOTAL __19__

WEDNESDAY __10th__

Felt great again!

PACE __7:48__ WEATHER __15°__ DISTANCE __5__ WEEK TOTAL __24__

THURSDAY _11th_

Too cold and windy

PACE _8:17_   WEATHER _20° Wind_   DISTANCE _8_   WEEK TOTAL _32_

FRIDAY _12th_

Easy day.

PACE _7:49_   WEATHER _28°_   DISTANCE _4_   WEEK TOTAL _36_

SATURDAY _13th_

Longest run in 3 months.

PACE _8:32_   WEATHER _30°_   DISTANCE _14_   WEEK TOTAL _(50)_

SUMMARY

No real problem with a
50-mile week. Move to 55.

WEEKS TOTAL _50 mi_   LONGEST RUN _14 mi_   SHORTEST RUN _4 mi_

AVERAGE RUN _7.1_   MONTHS TOTAL _81_   YEARS TOTAL _81_

DAILY WEIGHT		MORNING PULSE	
	Wed _145_		Wed _55_
Sun _145_	Thurs _144_	Sun _56_	Thurs _56_
Mon _146_	Fri _144_	Mon _54_	Fri _54_
Tues _145_	Sat _143_	Tues _54_	Sat _54_

Pay for It

Let's hope you aren't one of those who derive your motivation from financial commitment. If you are, pay for stress tests, body-fat tests, blood tests, X-rays, and regular checkups; take private lessons, order Finnish running shoes, buy a pulse meter, and get a custom tailored warm-up suit and gear bag; purchase the complete works of Joe Henderson; and donate a new locker room/sauna to your running club. That should keep you running for a little while.

Buddy System

Making a pact with a spouse, friend, or coworker can be strong medicine. It helps to find someone who progresses at the same rate you do.

Etcetera

- Tape a picture of yourself running to the refrigerator door.
- Set your running shoes by the front door at night.
- Wear your running shoes to bed at night.
- Subscribe to *Runner's World.*
- Don't allow yourself to read the paper until you've run in the morning (afternoon).
- Promise yourself a new car (vacation, house, divorce) after you've run 1,000 miles.
- Purchase a non-refundable ticket to Boston for the marathon one year in advance.

OVER MOTIVATION

Fortunately, compulsive, overly competitive running behavior is not as common or as hazardous as some feared. Dr. Meyer Friedman, for one, predicted one heart-attack death for every 10,000 miles jogged caused by the so-called type A individuals overdoing it.

The competitive type As can, however, cause some problems for themselves. If you find yourself wanting to overtake anyone

The buddy system

running ahead of you, if you find yourself refusing to drop off the pace when running with superior runners, or if you are frequently dissatisfied with your progress, you may be headed for injuries or you may burn out on running.

Sports psychologist Tom Tutko has encountered such behavior numerous times. If you notice such super-competitive
tendencies in yourself, he has this advice for you:

- run alone.
- write out a schedule, a reasonable running program, and
  don't exceed it.
- don't compete.
- make a six-month commitment.

IMPROVING

Veteran runners need motivation too. How many runners
plod at a pace far below their potential? It is quite possible to
fall into the habit of jogging less strenuously than needed to
produce cardiovascular fitness benefits.

What motivates someone to work toward a nine-minute pace,
then an eight, then seven? Why would 80,000 people a year run
26.2 miles at a stretch? Why would someone in their sixties try
a 440 sprint? Once you've gotten hooked on running, your
quest for personal excellence is the only thing you can count on
to keep you pushing your limits.

If you feel your running has been in a rut for a good while,
your best bet is a Joe Henderson book. *Jog, Run, Race* or *Run
Farther, Run Faster* in particular will have you shedding
minutes and adding miles in no time.

Improvement Checklist

The value running has for most people lies outside running
itself. That is, satisfaction is derived from the improved quality
of daily life, not from trophies, medals, or records.

While you are improving your running, your running should
be improving you. Here are some questions to ask yourself from
time to time.

- Am I more effective at work? Am I producing more and
  better work?
- Do I feel sharper, more alert, more vigorous?

- Am I sleeping better? In fewer hours?
- Am I eating better?
- Do I feel more confident, more capable?
- Do I get along with others better? Am I more relaxed?
- Do I feel healthier? Freer from minor ailments?

We make young colts out of old 45s.
　　　　　—Sign in North American Rockwell Gym

Chapter 4

Workouts and Work

In 1894, National Cash Register in Ohio, thanks to the efforts of John Patterson, began a program of twice-a-day exercise breaks for employees. The Indian Packing Company of Green Bay, Wisconsin, fielded a football team of employees, now evolved into the Green Bay Packers. Such incidents of employer-sponsored fitness programs in the United States have been isolated until recently. Even where they did occur, they were usually established only for a select group of young males.

Now, more than three hundred major corporations—Exxon, McGraw-Hill, Weyerhauser, Merrill Lynch, Pepsico, Memorex, General Foods, Kimberly Clark, Firestone, and Boeing, to name a few—and several hundred smaller companies sponsor employee fitness programs.

DOLLARS AND CENTS

The companies that have hesitated to implement fitness programs have usually wanted to see proof that their efforts would make a dent into the 200 billion dollars spent annually for health care (40 percent of which is borne by Business), into the 3 billion dollars spent each year on Workmans' Compensation, into the 35 billion that heart attacks cost Business each year.

The first thorough description of a corporate fitness program was only published in 1974; there simply hasn't been time to compile the data over enough years to verify the savings-to-cost ratio for physical fitness programs.

The Figures So Far

North American Life will publish the first major fitness-program evaluation in 1980. Their preliminary data indicates dramatic improvements in such categories as absenteeism, morale, and productivity directly owing to the fitness program.
Other studies have shown such facts as:

Absenteeism. Occidental Life found that regular users of the company gym were absent half as often as non-users. Swedish studies found the same reduction in absenteeism.

Productivity. In a University of Minnesota study of commercial pilots, 60 percent of the group taking part in physical activity reported "greater capacity to work harder both mentally and physically." Russian studies of assembly-line productivity have pointed to a 2- to 5-percent boost among regular exercisers, sometimes going as high as 15 percent.

Sickness. There is evidence that regular exercisers suffer flus and colds one-third as often as non-exercisers (one-sixth among middle-aged and older) and have lighter bouts when they do come down ill.

Work Quality. A Russian report on textile workers showed 31 percent fewer errors once a fitness program was implemented.

Medical Costs. Companies with comprehensive exercise programs have frequently been able to point to health-care costs rising at half the national average (about 12 percent).

The Race to Keep Up

Many of the companies that have joined the rush to providing exercise programs and facilities for employees decided they could no longer wait for the statistics to be published. They have been motivated by such models as Japanese industry, where physical exercise is an integral part of the work day and where productivity is unrivaled by any other nation.

Toyota, to name one example, provides a 14 million dollar facility, not just to employees, but to the public as well. Productivity at Toyota exceeds that of American auto manufacturers *by a factor of five,* much of which has been attributed to greater health and morale among Japanese workers.

Feedback

Even once the actuarial tables are published, the best criterion for consideration of a company-sponsored fitness program will still be the responses of those who have participated. The most-cited case is the 1968 National Aeronautics and Space Administration (NASA) year-long program involving executives aged 35 to 55.

NASA offered 259 men the opportunity to participate in exercise sessions three times a week. At the end of the study, half the regular participants reported improved performance and attitude at work. Nearly all claimed they felt better and had improved stamina. Half reported sounder sleep, and more than half lost weight. Many who smoked quit or cut back. These results were echoed by the occasional participants, though not to the same degree.

In order of frequency, here are the most common effects cited by participants in the NASA program:

1. decrease in food consumption
2. more positive work attitude
3. less stress and tension
4. improved work performance
5. more selective in kind of food consumed
6. increased physical activity beyond the program
7. expanded recreational activities
8. more adequate sleep and rest
9. reduction in smoking
10. improved sexual relations.

Xerox found the incidence of alcohol, tobacco, and drug use much reduced among participants in their program. They also found 90 percent of the participants reporting increased work capacity.

Further feedback comes from the top executives of companies with programs. W. W. Keeler, Chairman of the Board at Phillips Petroleum, sums it up when he says, "For most of us, the benefits of a physical conditioning program go beyond more productive individuals. They live longer and happier lives. When we consider the investment our companies have in people and our reliance on their skills and experience, it is clear that the longevity of employees is a real benefit to our organization."

IMPLEMENTING THE PROGRAM

The reason for including a chapter such as this is that many of the readers of a book directed to those over 40 will be in positions of authority where they work. If your employer offers a fitness program, you should take advantage of it. If no program is available where you work, you may want to get one started.

Individual Programs

How you go about starting a conditioning program will depend on whether you are Chairman of the Board of one of *Fortune*'s 500, a shipping clerk, owner of your own small business, or what. The shape your program takes will depend on available finances, facilities, promotion, top-management backing, and so on.

Fitness programs vary even wider than the range of businesses, unions, community groups, etcetera, that offers them. Xerox and Kimberly Clark provide facilities costing more than two million dollars while companies as large as Memorex and Hewlett-Packard run successful programs without facilities.

Many companies, such as Weyerhauser, charge employees and their families a nominal fee for membership in a fitness club. Some companies bear the entire cost, some subsidize memberships in commercial fitness clubs, some merely provide time allowances, such as an extra half hour at lunch, for those who want to pursue their own routine.

Some companies provide access to a gym at any time of the

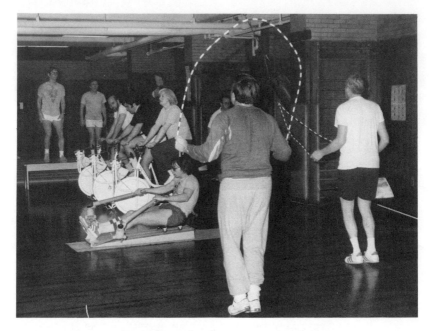

A workout in the company gym

day. Others offer regular exercise breaks. Some offer programs outside company hours only.

Some companies promote their programs heavily, even as part of their recruitment program. Participation in some programs runs over 90 percent, in others, less than 1 percent. Some companies provide separate facilities for men and women or for different levels of management and staff. Some companies do just fine without even providing shower facilities.

For detailed information on all the considerations that go into particularizing a fitness program, consult *Organizing Fitness Programs* by Don T. Jacobs.

Common Elements

Despite the variety in programs two things are common to all successful programs: management backing and leadership. Without management backing, programs have almost no chance of growing larger than a few already-fit individuals making use of the facilities to maintain their fitness. The less fit are reluctant to try to break into such cliques.

When only a small group participates—and this is a very real concern of small companies—there is the slight possibility that a freak accident could more than offset the long-term good of the program. The feedback is that exercise programs work best and benefit the company most when participation is wide-spread.

If you don't hold decision-making power where you work, you may have to settle for a clique at first. Organize others who share your interest, seek new members, and gradually try to formalize.

The issue of accidents brings us to the second common element—leadership. As a practical necessity, a company should put the program under the charge of a competent physical instructor. The instructor (or instructors) should be able to individualize training for all types of fitness, diet, and personality characteristics; they should be versed in CPR and other life-saving techniques; and they should have the gift for getting people motivated. This would hold true whether your instructor is a part-time consultant or a staff capable of everything from medical screening to lectures to physical therapy. Competent leadership reduces the risk of accident and injury.

Fitness vs. Recreation

Sometimes fitness program planning runs afoul of an aging president who decides to allocate the funds to a skeet range, bowling alley, or fishing boat. To derive the benefits listed, you must implement a fitness program of aerobic exercise. Recreational programs are fine as an adjunct.

Programs that don't offer running as the central activity usually offer swimming, indoor or outdoor circuit training (see chapter 14), rowing or exercycle apparatus, racquetball, or other strenuous exercise.

CORPORATE CUP ASSOCIATION

The Corporate Cup Association was founded by *Runner's World* Publisher Bob Anderson to further employee fitness and to provide an outlet for friendly competition beyond the college

The Corporate Cup Relays

level. The CCA sponsors, among its many activities, the Corporate Cup Relays.

The seven regional relay meets attracted 170 companies in 1979, the inaugural year. Ten teams from each regional qualified for the nationals held in Berkeley, California, in August. Sixty-three corporations, large and small, took part in the nationals.

Relay Events

The events are designed to require wide participation among member-company employees. The eight events are

1. Open Relay—five employees run a three-mile, two-mile, two one-mile, and a half-mile leg.

2. Pyramid Relay—five runners do a quarter, half, three-quarter, half, and quarter.

3. Women's Relay—three women run a two-mile, one-mile, and half-mile leg.

4. Master's Relay—three employees at least 40 years old run two miles, one mile, and a half mile.

5. Executive Relay—four executives (must meet classification guidelines) run two miles, one mile, a half, and a quarter.

6. 10K Road Race—five runners, first three score.

7. One-Mile Team Track—three runners; score is total of top two.

8. President's Relay—three in the corporate hierarchy run one-mile, half-mile, and quarter-mile legs.

First Year's Results

The national finals of the Corporate Cup Relays provided a splendid format for competition among companies. Many personal records were set. Many there appreciated the opportunity to take to the track against the likes of Derek Clayton, Bill Clark, Amby Burfoot, and other world-class runners who now are Captains of Industry.

The final rankings were:

Place	Team	Score
1	Pacific Gas & Electric	85
2	General Electric	76
3	Pacific Telephone	64
4	Texas Instruments	48
5	Delta Airlines	35
6	*Runner's World* Magazine	34
7	Bankers Trust	29
8	Athletic Annex	28
9	Hewlett Packard	27
10	American Telephone & Telegraph	25

Participation in the CCA costs a firm an annual fee of $250, no matter the number of employees or division, (unless the divisions simply want to compete separately). Teams who earn places in the finals receive a share of a $35,000 travel fund. In short, the CCA provides a very inexpensive way to lend challenge and excitement to any corporate fitness program—by testing the results against what other companies have achieved.

Further information on CCA programs can be obtained from

Corporate Cup Association
1400 Stierlin Road
Mountain View, California   94043

Chapter 5

Time Priorities
Alex Ratelle

A special problem for the over-40 runner is time priorities. Just as some well-entrenched habits are helpful in the longtime survival of a running program, other habits act to inhibit and frequently interfere with finding time for a daily workout.

A good example of the latter is our career ambitions. These often start at a very early age, become embedded in work routines and propel us toward job advancement. At first, career goals are of our own manufacture, encouraged and perhaps molded by our parents. But as time progresses we find our peers, teachers, and others urging us onward and upward. Soon we are watching clocks from hour-to-hour, aiming for promotions from year-to-year, and all the while struggling to find time for a day's play in our hectic schedules.

How we spend our time becomes of increasing interest and concern to a spreading network of individuals, groups, and corporations. Where the ends are shared, there is little conflict.

But when people dependent on our presence or productivity see us disappearing in our running gear at odd hours toward odd places, they are apt to be concerned. Sometimes these people react with dark intimations that we are somehow losing not only time but also energy, wealth, and—more vaguely—elements of our personality and temperament.

Expectations

All humans, all of us, live in a world of images. We have images of ourselves and of others. These images are imbedded in a complex of those thousands, and millions even, of factors that form us, our present, and our future.

The runner is certainly not immune from the images of those in his immediate environment. When we veer from our path at middle age and participate in activities that do not fit a standard or acceptable form, we challenge the comfortable and established image that our friends and colleagues have of us.

With the growing interest in running and related activities, it is becoming simpler to explain ourselves. And we can now point to examples at hand.

But this does not completely explain ourselves to everyone. And some of our intimates remain uncomfortable and distressed.

I have found it best not to elaborate on my views of running, and its merits for the middle aged. But to let my example do most of the speaking for me. My program has come to be a matter of faith with me. And how can you explain that to a pagan? At a cocktail party?

I have found that it is best not to discuss my immediate running plans when suiting up. This has become so successful that even when the living room is full of the odors of dinner my children will step over my prostrate stretching form to get the evening paper without uttering a single comment. This is a special victory, because all six of my children know that dinner will not be served until Dad returns from his run. And they have learned that Dad has the stamina, desire, and malevolence to convert a one-hour run to a two-hour run if they challenge or anger him. I can't recommend this strategy to every runner but it does show that families adapt easily to consistent behavior and consistent schedules.

Avoiding Friction

The demands of my practice, my occupation, my family and my community are essentially no different than they are for anyone else my age. My life is frequently frenetic and fatiguing.

I sometimes stretch my systems to the breaking point. It is then that I become quite cautious in appraising or judging the reactions of intimates to my "private" life, my "secret" life, my running.

Recently a friend asked me how I was able to find the time to run more than 100 miles a week. Then, before giving me a chance to respond, he injected that I was surely depriving my family and friends of my companionship by spending "all that time on the road."

My entire running program, I told him, requires less than the normal adult in my community spends getting his daily television fix. My entire weekend of "long mileage" consumes less time than a single round of golf or three sets of tennis and far less than two football games. That golfers, tennis players, and professional sports fans do not recognize this in runners, nor honor it, does not detract from the simple truth that running does not consume a lot of time, certainly not when compared with the huge chunks of time devoured by so many other pastimes. Yes, I admit that I want an hour a day for my workout, but that is less than 5 percent of a day and it does not represent a major work or familial disruption.

Nonrunners

The counter-system critic and/or cynic is adroit in his commentary on running and its benefits. Perhaps because he has no "daily run" himself he has more time and energy to devote to observations about running in general and your success in particular.

"How did you do at Boston this year?" is a common opener. Whether the response is made by Gary Bjorklund, "Fifth," or Alex Ratelle,"Nine hundred and twenty-fifth," their reply will inevitably be, "Oh, that's too bad." I cannot imagine what Bill Rodgers receives in the way of malignant consolation when he answers with, "First."

It is perhaps one of the great rewards of running, that after a time, the over-all place becomes of small consequence. Unlike many skill sports, merely finishing is the goal. And of course to finish among and with friends who are runners is not only reward but comfort. And whatever veneer covers our ambition for a "big win," this is scraped away in the first moments after the gun goes off. We sweat and strain to hold a position in the phalanx that God never intended us to hope for. And we are comforted and reassured by our level of discernible pain that we are indeed doing everything possible to preserve not only our position but our honor and pride. And a permanent imprint is made in our brain that we are giving our utmost.

To expect our nonrunning friends to understand the complex of emotions and commitment we associate with our running is certainly unreasonable. Human judgment and assessment is based on knowledge and experience. The nonrunner has had of necessity to absorb his knowledge from hearsay and the media. Which amounts to little knowledge indeed. And as to experience he must refer back to some remote time in past history when he too strained and hurt to gain a finish line, goaded by coach, family, and friends to nausea, pain, and physiological and mental revolt.

We are surrounded by a lifestyle that is hostile, unhealthy, unwise, and when viewed from any perspective, downright foolish. We have, over a long period of time and with some effort, found "another way." Be patient with the friends, relatives, critics, and general unbelievers, for they too are looking for their way out. And from the sharply increasing numbers of people with exercise programs, we may safely assume that some large quantity of bread has been cast upon the waters.

Ironically, I remember that no relatives or friends raised questions about my cramped schedule when, in my young professional career, my community asked me to be on 24-hour call for days on end. Nor, for that matter, did they ask about my state of health. But now that I'm using my first spare time since childhood to enjoy the excitement of running and to take care of my physical and psychological needs, my motives become suspect.

So at the bottom line, it comes down to what we think of our time, our responsibilities and how we would use ourselves up before our cup is emptied. Forever.

Running quickly comes to teach us our own mortality and

leads to a greater appreciation of ourselves and the limited time at our disposal. Running seems to me, in this regard, a uniquely humanizing experience. As we progress along the road, a pattern develops. We come to know what we need. We also come to understand what others may legitimately expect of us. We learn how to look at the puzzle of life, how to distinguish the pieces—job, family, self—and how to choose to arrange them. There's plenty of room for all.

Alex Ratelle, a physician whose practice is in Edina, Minnesota, is the fastest over-50 marathoner in the United States. Portions of this chapter appeared previously in Runner's World.

Part Two

Training

Chapter 6

Training Principles

Training is nothing more than the course you must follow to accustom your body to new activity. A forty year old who decided to give up a marathon lifestyle in favor of the typical sedentary lifestyle would have to go through training just as much as someone doing the reverse. It takes time to build up to a pack of cigarettes a day. Four hours of uninterrupted television watching in the beginning is a challenge to the restless marathoner. And the new convert might have to settle for a convenience-food meal every other day at first before building to three sub-nutritious meals a day.

The beginners training program in chapter 7 is devised around the more or less universal rate at which individuals adjust to major changes in their activity. In general, for the first six to eight weeks the body will be resisting you, trying to talk you out of subjecting it to the stress of change, whether that change is learning to run or learning to smoke tobacco. The body responds with pain, stiffness, and general stubbornness to attempts to get it out of its rut.

During the next twenty weeks, the body decides you are not going to leave it alone and begins to go along with you. At the end of twenty-six weeks, you will be "positively addicted," as the psychologists say, to your running program. You will have developed a level of energy that is yours to use to maintain or improve your fitness for the rest of your life. This is your "base," a degree of stamina and ability which is yours, which can be maintained with less work than it took to obtain it, and which is your foundation for progressing as a runner. (More about this later.)

When any good-sized group of people launch into an uncharted activity, certain insights, refinements, and efficiencies are bound to be discovered. In the case of running, coaches, physicians, researchers, and individual runners have contributed to the store of our knowledge about training—what it takes to get the biggest return on your running investment. Running can be pursued in ways that will guarantee you get very little fitness out of it, and it can be pursued in suicidal fashion that will wreck your body more than improve it. It makes sense to understand and benefit from the discoveries others have made— to save yourself some of the anguish others have put themselves through (and will continue to put themselves through) needlessly.

PRINCIPLE OF STRESS

Stress, in manageable amounts, is the stimulus that provokes a training response. It must be regular and strong enough to stimulate adaptation, but it cannot come in such heavy and frequent doses that it overwhelms the adaptation system causing a breakdown. Running itself is only one of many stresses acting on a runner. Others are faulty diet, psychic unrest, and environmental insults such as extreme heat or cold. Runners must consider the stress-load as a whole and adapt to it.

PRINCIPLE OF OVERLOAD

"Overload" isn't the same as "overwork." Overloading is selective stressing—enough to stimulate the desired response without producing exhaustion.

Forbes Carlile says, "The training load must be severe and must be applied frequently enough and with sufficient intensity to cause the body to adapt maximally to a particular activity." But he adds, "It is at the same time true that sustained all-out efforts in training or in races should be made only sparingly."

This is what New Zealand coach Arthur Lydiard meant by his now-famous advice: "Train, don't strain." No results can come without training, but on the other hand straining too hard or often is self-defeating.

PRINCIPLE OF SPECIFICITY

The system adapts to the specific exercise given. Walk, and you become fit for walking. Bicycle, and you become a better cyclist. Run, and you get in shape for running. Walking may be a good prelude to running, but it will not make you a runner.

Many activities can give you general fitness, but complex muscle movements do not transfer readily from one activity to the next. If your goal is to excel in a given activity, your training will need to resemble that activity.

Many runners who try their hand at cycling (and vice versa) have been hobbled for days by failure to heed this principle. Thinking they can put exertion into the pedals equal to what they put in on the track, the runners cycle vigorously only to be greeted by screaming muscles unused to the work.

Stamina is not so specific. Running, for instance, can improve your stamina for all other sports, making allowance, however, for fatigue brought on by the use of previously little-used muscle groups.

PRINCIPLE OF REGULARITY

Almost any amount of running will provide fitness benefits if only it's done regularly. As little as ten minutes of running at 70 to 80 percent of your maximum every other day will do you good. Every day of layoff beyond one takes its toll.

Conditioning comes quickly. Every exercise session seems to show an improvement over previous performances. But conditioning also vanishes quickly. Come back slowly after any layoff, particularly one of more than a week. One study of the Danish Olympic crew showed that they completely lost their conditioning after one month of inactivity.

PRINCIPLE OF PROGRESSION

Obviously, progress is quickest and most apparent at the start, and it slows as one approaches his maximum potential. The more progress, the harder new improvements are to achieve. Elite runners put in more work to shave a fraction of a second off their time than beginning runners do to cut several minutes.

Progress does not follow a smooth upward curve. There is a "plateau effect," periods of rapid improvement are followed by a stagnant period. This can be observed both short term and long term. Often, two or three labored runs will be followed by an easy, free-flowing run only to be followed by more labored runs. And a relatively slow month might be followed by a couple of weeks of rapid progress in turn followed by weeks of relatively little improvement. A runner has to be prepared to work through these periods of no apparent improvement, waiting for the spurts of progress.

PRINCIPLE OF DIMINISHING RETURNS

The first mile is the most helpful as far as conditioning goes. Each succeeding one gives less benefit than the one before. In other words, runners work more and more for less and less.

The same is true over the long haul as mentioned in the preceding discussion. As Hal Higdon puts it, "It doesn't take much to get 90 percent fitness—only a few miles a day. But it takes progressively more training as you get close to your ultimate potential, until at the very highest levels you're putting in a huge investment for a very small gain."

But Higdon notes, "It's the small gains that make the difference between winning and losing."

PRINCIPLE OF RECOVERY

The interval system (see chapter 14) has more meaning to it than simply mixing fast and slow running in a workout. The principle of alternating effort with recovery and rest applies to all training, regardless of the specific method used.

You need time to rest between training sessions. The rest is not merely a passive state; it is a time when your body is busily adapting to the stress you have put it through.

Most runners feel that stacking a training program with a mix of hard and easy days does more good than a same-every-day program. Hard training sessions should be followed by a day of complete rest and several days of light workouts before another hard training session is attempted.

PRINCIPLE OF SEASONS

Those of you who race must realize that racing places a heavy debit on your fitness investment. It is just as easy to exhaust the body as it is to exhaust a bank account. Long periods free of races and hard training runs are necessary in order for the body to build up its fitness investment.

Training hard is not possible year-round. Those who desire to exceed 80 percent of their maximum should build up carefully, limit their peak work to two to four all-out runs in the course of a couple of months, then allow three or four months of training at no more than 80 percent of maximum.

Marathon runners will probably find that they fare better by running their races in clusters of two or three (with at least three weeks rest between races) followed by at least three race-free months spent building up to the next season of effort.

PRINCIPLE OF PACING

Run fast, run short; run slow, run long. The faster you run, the more demand you place on the less-efficient anaerobic energy system, and the sooner you give out. The slower you run, the more you utilize the aerobic system—a system that has been put to the test in 100-mile ultramarathons, in 48-hour races, in three-day runs, and every other kind of brutal endurance test, all without fail.

Set the pace according to the distance of the run. But also set it according to the length of your desired running career. Too many races at too fast a pace can burn you out.

PRINCIPLE OF INDIVIDUALITY

This is the principle that states both that no program that is right for someone else will be entirely right for you and that no program designed for you should be followed too rigidly—make allowances for unexpected peak days or down days. The important consideration here is to determine whether your program is causing you to adjust to progressively increasing amounts of strain or whether it is causing your body to gradually lose its ability to adjust itself.

At the outset, beginning runners have little choice but to follow the advice of others. However, as they learn more about themselves, they will be better able to adapt their training program to suit their own needs.

There is obviously a great deal of interrelation among these training principles. The common theme seems to be that you should push yourself, but do it a little at a time. Follow these principles to get the most benefit from your running program and to make sure you can keep running for the rest of your life.

Chapter 7

Workouts I

The principles listed in the previous chapter are broad enough to cover fitness joggers and competitive racers, beginners and veterans. The next several chapters will offer more specific training guidelines for beginners, intermediates, and veterans, for fitness runners and competitive runners.

TRAINING SESSIONS

Each training session, whether your first or your ten thousandth, should include a relaxation period, a warm-up, an aerobic workout, and a cool-down period.

Relaxation Period

Take two minutes to lie down and relax, or stroll and let your mind go blank. While most runners impatiently neglect this stage, it's a good idea to relax your shoulders, limber your legs, and breathe deeply before running.

Warm-up Period

The best warm-up is a short walk or jog to raise the temperature of the muscles followed by stretching exercises. (See chapter 9 for information on stretching). Warning: No matter how flexible you are, you need to stretch prior to exercising.

Increased flexibility is one of the benefits of stretching, but the main reason for stretching is to warm and loosen the muscles before exerting them. Running on muscles that are cool and tight is an invitation to tears and pulls.

Warm-ups increase in importance with age. When heavy exercise is begun suddenly, the heart may not be resupplied with blood as quickly as it pumps blood out. In older or unconditioned persons, that lag can lead to cardiac ischemia—erratic pumping of the heart that could trigger a heart attack.

All muscles, including the heart, function more efficiently when taken gradually to their work level. Never neglect your warm-up, and start your workout slowly, picking up the pace over the first few hundred yards.

Aerobic Workout

The aerobic phase of a training session is the part that provides the fitness benefits. It is accomplished by maintaining any activity that can hold your heart rate above 50 percent of maximum for twenty minutes or longer. For the purposes of this book, walking, jogging, and running are the aerobic activities.

All one has to do to fulfill the aerobic phase of a workout is to exercise at a pace that will keep the heart rate within the target range, picking up the pace if the heart rate dips out of the range and slowing down if the heart rate rises above the range. Monitoring of the pulse is necessary at first but can be dispensed with as one gets familiar with the levels of exertion.

Cool-Down Period

Muscles that are worked hard and not allowed to cool down gradually are prone to stiffness and soreness. After the aerobic workout, walk a few hundred yards then repeat the stretching exercises you did during the warm-up. For one thing, such activity will help rid the muscles of wastes trapped between the fibers. Following the cool-down period with another relaxation period is a good practice.

WHERE TO WORK OUT

Every runner quickly establishes preferences in the location of workouts. These preferences sort themselves out into three rather evenly divided groups with a special fourth group.

Track

Running on a track appeals to the runner who likes to "keep track" of distance and time. The track provides a convenient standard.

A track gives you more contact with other runners

Benefits:

- Ease of calculating distances covered.
- Fellowship. There are always plenty of other runners these days.
- Atmosphere. Many people just feel like running once at the track. The track provides a context for running.
- Facilities. Showers, lockers, and drinking water are always at hand.

Drawbacks:

- Boredom. Many are they who cannot put up with the monotony of endless laps.
- Inconvenient. Crowding, the need to drive there and back, limited hours, and even fees are some of the obstacles encountered now and then with tracks.

Cross-Country

What could be better than running over hill and dale, through green meadows, and along peaceful streams? Many runners demand beautiful scenery for their eyes and thick grass for their feet. Running across golf courses would be ideal if it weren't for the damned balls flying around.

Benefits:

- Peace and solitude. You can't beat scenic surroundings for a relaxing run.
- Injury Prevention. The foot's impact on grass is much less than on road or track surfaces.

Drawbacks:

- Lack of availability. As much as some urban dwellers prefer countryside for their running, it's just not convenient on a daily basis.
- Lack of facilities. In case you dry out, suffer an injury, or need to relieve yourself, there's seldom a facility around.
- Injuries. The possibility of tripping and twisting an ankle in the process increases.

Running on country roads

Roads

Running on roads in our paved society means running just about anywhere. As soon as you're out your door, you're on the run. Given the choice between concrete and asphalt, take asphalt, its much easier on the feet.

Benefits:

- Convenience. The whole country is your running course.

Drawbacks:

- Injuries. Roads are notoriously hard on the feet (and body if you take a spill).
- Distractions. Looking out for curbs, pot holes, dogs, cars, bicycles, and so on can diminish the relaxation value of running.

If you want to run on roads, stay away from traffic. Exhaust fumes are poisonous. The main menace is carbon monoxide, which fortunately does disperse quickly. For comfort and safety, stay at least twenty yards from light traffic and fifty yards from heavy traffic. Run on side streets, alleys, parking lots—anything to avoid exhaust fumes.

Indoors

A special case is running indoors. Serious runners living in regions subject to severe winter weather would be well advised to hunt out the nearest gym, barn, or coliseum that offers protection against blizzards.

When the weather is bad enough to keep you housebound, try jump rope. There are several indoor exercise books on the market that offer all sorts of possibilities for maintaining fitness when you can't get outdoors.

You will quickly make your own choices about where you want to run (if you don't have them already). Some prefer a different course every day for variety. Others prefer to run the same course each time, the better to judge their improvement. Some like hills; others like it level. Some prefer to run laps around the block so they are never too far from home should they decide to hang it up early. Others find the only way to get in long distance is to run off to a distant destination so there is little choice but to run back.

Many metropolitan areas now have booklets available on the best local running courses. Check your book store if you live in a large city.

WHEN TO WORK OUT

As a practical matter, it makes little difference what time of the day you exercise. Here are some considerations:

- Avoid the heat of the day in warm weather.
- Seek the heat of the day in cold weather.
- Running before breakfast may increase the release of growth hormone, which has a beneficial effect on the body's healing process.

A treadmill allows you to run indoors

- Avoid running in the dark for obvious safety reasons.
- Run at least an hour before eating or two hours afterward.
- For the weight-conscious, running before the largest meal tends to suppress appetite.
- Running at noon can prevent the afternoon blahs.

Some prefer to run before work so as to be more alert. Others prefer to run after work to relax from the tensions of the day. Some serious runners advocate twice-a-day workouts. Again, your own preferences will reveal themselves quickly.

HOW LONG TO WORK OUT

Runners quickly note a sequence of bodily sensations akin to the shifting of gears in an automobile. First gear lasts for the first minute or so until the body begins to sweat. Second gear is an uncomfortable period of short breath that lasts for the first mile or two. Third gear is commonly known as "second wind." Fourth gear comes after thirty to forty minutes when the body begins to oxidize fats as well as sugars. And the grinding of gears occurs at about twenty miles when the body runs out of sugars to burn.

You must get into third gear and stay there for ten minutes or more to get complete fitness benefits. That means you should run at least twenty minutes. Every now and then, particularly if you want to lose weight, crank on up to fourth gear with a run of forty-five minutes or longer.

Chapter 8

Workouts II

The second most important goal of a workout, after the fitness benefits, is obtaining feedback on your fitness level. This is particularly so in the beginning. And if you are the type to keep a training diary, you will want to keep careful track throughout your running career.

PULSE

Your pulse rate will give you your most direct feedback on your exercise level. The three pulse rates you will need to monitor are resting pulse rate, exercise heart rate, and recovery heart rate. The fourth rate you will need to be aware of is maximum pulse rate.

Maximum Pulse Rate

Let's assume you are not going to have a lab test of your maximum oxygen uptake and maximum pulse rate. It will be sufficient, then, to estimate your maximum pulse rate, the so-called theoretical maximum pulse rate. That will work for about four out of five people, with the rest varying by less than 10 percent, except for the well-conditioned, who likely will have lower maximums.

The formula for computing your theoretical maximum is this:

$$TMPR = 220 - age$$

If you are forty, your max would be 180. At age eighty, your maximum is 140. The value of knowing this figure is in determining your target range for exercise heart rate. Once you have a few months' experience running, you can check your maximum rate by running at a rate that will bring you to exhaustion in three to six minutes and checking your pulse then.

Exercise Heart Rate

To get any fitness benefits, you must exceed 50 percent of max, and you cannot exceed 100 percent. The usual target range is 70 to 85 percent.

You get fit by continuing an activity that will keep your heart rate in the target range for twenty to thirty minutes. For those quite out of shape, 50 to 60 percent of max will do for starters. Beginners should try 60 to 70 percent. Normal ranges are 70 to 85 percent (see below). Speed training takes place from 85 to 95 percent. Above 95 percent represents the final kick in a race.

Resting Pulse Rate

Another way of computing your target exercise heart rate is to multiply your resting heart rate by two. This is less satisfactory since there is greater variation among individuals in the resting rate than in the maximum rate. Once you know your resting rate, you can check to see if your target exercise rates as computed each way (75 percent of max and two times resting) are roughly equal.

Your resting heart rate is the lowest rate your heart achieves. Consequently, the best time to determine it is first thing on awakening. Well-conditioned athletes have recorded resting heart rates in the thirties! As your heart improves its stroke volume, it will likewise be able to do the same work with fewer strokes.

One of the most reliable checks you can make is for next-day fatigue using resting heart rate. If, first thing in the morning, your resting pulse is 10 percent or more above average, you overdid it the day before and should adjust the new day's training accordingly.

Recovery Heart Rate

The recovery heart rate is a doublecheck you should make one minute after the end of the aerobic workout. If by that time your pulse rate hasn't returned to within four or five beats of its preworkout level, you need to cut back on the time and effort expended.

Taking Your Pulse

There are gadgets on the market for up to $150 solely for taking your pulse with. A watch capable of counting off the seconds will do.

For resting heart rate, as soon as your eyes are able to focus in the morning, take your pulse on your neck or wrist for one-half minute and multiply by two (use your middle and ring fingers to ckeck pulse—the thumb has a pulse of its own that may interfere with your reading. On the wrist, the pulse can best be located on the thumb side).

For exercise heart rate, take a pulse before starting the warm-up phase, before starting the aerobic phase, four or five times during the aerobic phase, immediately on completing the aerobic phase, and, for the recovery heart rate, one minute after cessation of activity. In these cases, take a ten-second count and multiply by six, the reason being that heart rate begins to recover downward quickly. Since your heart will be pounding, you may find it simplest to place your hand over your chest for a pulse reading.

The following chart gives typical target exercise ranges for over-forty runners based on a ten-second count.

Age	10-second count	Age	10-second count
40-44	21-25	54-62	19-23
45-47	20-25	63-69	18-22
48-53	20-24	70-up	17-21

If your measured exercise rate is above or below your target figure, you'll need to reduce or pick up your pace accordingly. When recovering from a heavy workout, you may want to set a range lower than listed above. Later, once your base is established and you undertake speedwork, your ranges will go higher than above.

MAXIMUM OXYGEN UPTAKE

Maximum oxygen uptake, capacity, or consumption, as it is variously known, is an expression of a body's ability to use oxygen in the production of energy. It is stated in units of milliliters of oxygen consumed per kilogram of body weight per minute. Top middle-distance runners have uptakes of around 80, while the average American hovers around 30 to 40.

It is unlikely you will want to go to a biomechanical lab for a treadmill test of oxygen consumption. Very roughly, if you can run a nine-minute-plus mile, you're in the 30s; seven-plus, in the 40s; six-plus, in the 50s; five-plus, in the 60s; and under five, in the 70s and 80s.

BODY COMPOSITION

Assuming you don't want to go to a biomechanical lab to be weighed in a water tank or have calipers pinch various parts of your body, the best way to determine your proportion of body fat is to look at your naked body in a mirror.

FITNESS

Your maximum oxygen uptake is your best gauge of fitness. There are a few tests you can do on your own to give you an approximate indication, such as the Katch Step Test. You may find such tests valuable from time to time as a way of gauging your progress, particularly if you don't train on a standardized course.

Perhaps the simplest is the one formulated by Dr. Kenneth Cooper in *Aerobics*. Travel as far as you can in twelve minutes. For men and women over forty, covering less than one mile indicates poor condition, one to one-and-a-quarter miles fair, to one-and-a-half miles good, and more than one-and-a-half miles excellent.

If you try this test before starting your running program, don't go out with the idea of setting a state track record. Stop and walk if you get winded; don't overdo it for the sake of a better opinion of your condition than your condition warrants.

BODILY FEEDBACK

Likely, those who would most appreciate this section took one look at this chapter and skipped to chapter 9. Many are just as impatient with stopwatches, track running, pulse checks, and the like as others are engrossed in diary keeping, knowing the distance and time of every run, and so on.

This section says you can trust your impressions. Research has confirmed this. Runners tested have shown the ability to estimate pulse, time run, distance run, level of fitness, all to within just a few percent of actual findings.

One runner even went so far as to state, "You will never learn to tell time as long as you wear a watch." This may represent the extreme view, but if you know runners who do not wear a watch, or if you are one yourself, you'll know the number of times they announce, "I'm off for a forty-five-minute run," and return in exactly that time, even if they run an unfamiliar route. The same is true for pulse; with a little experience you can tell through feel alone whether you are above or below your target range.

The best proposition for a new runner is to check times, distances, and pulse rates religiously for the first several weeks, dispensing with the checks as they come to trust their estimations. Even those who want to maintain a training diary will find this adequate, with the addition maybe of a time trial every couple of weeks.

Chapter 9

Stretching

Unless you have a fondness for pain, don't omit stretching before and after your aerobic workout. Soreness usually arrives twenty to forty hours after exercise at the end of an ugly chain of events—exertion causes muscle fatigue which prevents the muscle from relaxing which leads to poor fluid circulation within the muscle (local anemia) which causes pain which produces further contraction which increases the pain and so on.

Static stretches (such as yoga stretches) interrupt this chain of events and reduce soreness to a minimum.

Another pain syndrome runners can fall into comes from running on cool muscles. When muscles are exercised, they contract and relax repeatedly. The warmer the muscle, the more quickly it can contract *and* relax. When muscles are not allowed to relax thoroughly between contractions, the result is tightening of the muscle and soreness.

Ballistic stretches (calisthenics) prevent soreness of this type by warming the muscles gradually.

Whenever a muscle is contracted rapidly, its natural response is to shorten and tighten in order to resist the strain. This is a progressive effect, which means that, with time, your range of motion will actually decrease. Stretching can offset that.

In short, these are the reasons you stretch before and after running: (1) to reduce soreness to a minimum and (2) to counteract the muscle tightening that running causes. Anyone who says you stretch to increase your flexibility (and particularly anyone who tells you you can do without stretching if you are not concerned about flexibility) is not quite correct.

Stretching can increase flexibility over the long term just as running will decrease it over time. The amount of stretching most runners do is adequate to counteract the effects of running. Those seeking significant improvement in their range of movement will need a much more comprehensive stretching program than is listed here.

Running itself will often cause a dramatic increase in freedom of movement, particularly for those who begin running after years of inactivity. However, don't be deceived. The new ease of movement is a short-term result of becoming more active. Without stretching, that ease of movement will be gradually reduced.

BALLISTIC STRETCHES

Most people refer to ballistic stretches as calisthenics or exercises and use the term "stretches" to mean only static stretches. However, ballistic stretches are most certainly *not* stretches when done incorrectly—they have the opposite effect.

Never bounce or jerk when doing calisthenics. If that advice is heeded, ballistic stretches are an important way to warm up for running. They should precede static stretches since static stretches are more beneficial when performed on warm muscles.

There are three other important cautions:

1. Do not do sit-ups with legs straight. That can lead to lower back pain. For the same reason, do not do straight leg lifts while lying on your back.
2. Do forward bends only *after* trunk twists and side bends. The latter relax the back; forward bends do not.
3. Keep the spine as straight as possible when bending forward or sideways. Bend from the hips, not from the waist. Arching and twisting motions are good for the spine; forward and sideways curving is not. If you must curve your back forward, curl down slowly, one vertebra at a time, so as not to jam the vertebrae into each other. Bending from the hips with the back straight is preferable.

Ballistic stretches play an important role in the warm-up for raising muscle temperature and increasing the heart rate gradually. How many repetitions you do of each exercise will depend on the weather. In general, these exercises have done their good when the first sweat appears; so fewer repetitions in warm weather, more in cool weather.

Remember: do not do these exercises so vigorously that you feel a bouncing or bobbing sensation in the muscles.

Warm-up Exercises

The order of the exercises below is based on increasing levels of exertion so as to raise the heart rate gradually.

1. *Neck Roll:* Twist and roll the head from side to side.
2. *Rowing:* Work the arms back and forth and around to loosen the shoulders.
3. *Lifts:* Raise on toetips.
4. *Twists:* Twist the trunk from one side to the other. When reaching the limit of stretch, use a purposeful motion—not a jerking motion.
5. *Forward bends:* Bend from the hips with back straight.
6. *Knee lifts:* Raise one knee and then the other.
7. *Knee bends:* Squat with back straight until legs reach a 90-degree bend.
8. *Straddle hops (jumping jacks):* Jump, spreading the legs out to the side and swinging the arms overhead. Jump again, closing the legs and bringing your arms to your sides.
9. *Jog in place or slow jog:* Continue at a slow pace until the first beads of sweat begin to form.

Those who want a more strenuous warm-up can include sit-ups, push-ups, chin-ups, and so forth. Many runners find it advantageous to do these sorts of exercises after running before the cool-down period.

STATIC STRETCHING

The most common class of traumatic running injury—tears and pulls—is caused this way: when a muscle is exposed to a sudden jerk, its automatic response is to recoil and resist the force. If the force is large enough, the muscle tears or is stretched violently.

A steadily increasing force on a muscle, on the other hand, bypasses the muscle's recoil mechanism. If the force (stretch) is maintained, the muscle relaxes and becomes more elastic— more able to "go with" sudden accidental forces.

Static stretches are the single most important adjunct to running; nothing beats them for preventing soreness and injuries. Don't skimp on this part of your warm-up and cool-down, and, since you are going to do them, do them correctly:

- Ease into the stretch. Jerky movements defeat your purpose.
- Hold the pose at least fifteen seconds, building slowly up to maximum stretch, maintaining it for a moment, then backing off just as slowly.
- Never hold your breath while stretching. Breathe deeply from the belly—not the chest.
- Maximum benefit comes when the muscles have been warmed prior to stretching.
- Take a moment to make certain your posture is correct before starting the stretch.

Remember also your individuality. Your range of motion on a particular stretch can vary significantly from that of others. Stretch according to what you feel, not according to what you see others do. Usually, when you reach maximum stretch, you will feel a pleasantly tight, burning sensation.

The Basic Runner's Stretches

The main areas of concern to runners are, of course, found in the legs: hamstrings, groin, quadriceps, calves, and Achilles tendons. Of the innumerable stretches for the various regions of your body and of the several different stretches for the areas just mentioned, we will limit this presentation to one stretch for each area. This is a *minimum*. You are encouraged to add more of your own.

Achilles stretch

From the ground up:

Achilles tendons: This stretch works on one leg at a time.
1. Stand about four feet in front of a wall, feet pointed straight ahead.
2. Lean forward, supporting yourself against the wall, and bring the inactive leg forward to a comfortable position.
3. Flex the knee of the rear leg slowly until you reach maximum stretch in the Achilles, hold, then back off slowly.
4. Repeat for the other leg.

Calf stretch

Calves: This stretch works best when the knees are locked.
1. Lower yourself a little closer to the wall than in the Achilles tendon stretch, feet pointed straight ahead.
2. Straighten the leg to be stretched and lock the knee (use thigh muscles to lift the patella upward).
3. Push the buttocks forward until you feel maximum stretch in the calf, hold, then back off slowly.
4. Repeat for other leg.

Quadriceps: The major muscles on the front of the thigh in most people are weak compared with the hamstrings, which oppose them, and need to be strengthened by running uphill, cycling, or lifting pails of rocks with the lower leg while sitting on the edge of a table. The quadriceps seldom lack a good

Quadriceps stretch

degree of flexibility but still need to be stretched before running.

1. Prop yourself against a wall with one arm.
2. Bend one leg up behind you and grasp the ankle with your free arm (it works somewhat better if you use the arm on the same side and pull slightly to the outside).
3. Lean forward at the hips as you pull against your leg until you feel the stretch in the front of your thigh.
4. Repeat for the other leg.

Hamstring stretch

Hamstrings: Most people's hamstrings are overly tight. They should get more attention than any other region in your stretching routine.

1. Prop one leg up on a bench, (a foot and a half high is about right; you don't need to raise your leg waist-high unless you are superflexible).
2. With toes pointed straight, hips even, and knees locked, lean forward from the hips until you feel the stretch in the back of your thigh.
3. After at least fifteen seconds, repeat with foot turned slightly inward and then again with the foot turned outward.
4. Repeat for other leg.

Groin stretch

*Groin:*Beginners should not overdo this one. Start out at five seconds of stretch and work up to fifteen.

1. Sit comfortably, back straight.
2. Bring your feet toward you until the soles touch six to ten inches in front of your crotch.
3. Press the knees toward the earth until you feel the stretch in your groin (the feeling may be more slight than in other stretches). As you get more proficient, you can push down on your knees with your hands.

Again, these are a minimum. See *New Exercises for Runners* if you want a more thorough program of stretches. Those interested in really improving their flexibility can find no better book than the *Runner's World Yoga Book.*

Chapter 10

Walking

America is getting back to its legs. There's no better evidence for this than the recent surge of interest in walking. Numerous books and articles have appeared in just the last year preaching the value of walking, and major running clubs, such as the New York Road Runners, have started walking programs. Many claim that the walking craze will surpass the jogging craze.

The so-called lost art of walking deserves the attention it has been getting. There *is* an art to it, one that offers many advantages to those who try it on whatever level. (There are basically four types of walking: strolling, brisk walking, jog-walking, and race walking. We'll be concerned with the last three.)

Some of the more obvious advantages include:

Fitness. Cardiovascular fitness may be increased without ever taking a running step. From the woefully out-of-shape beginners to the veteran marathoner, there is a level of walking that will provide a good workout.

Injuries. Walking ranks right alongside cycling and swimming as a way to come back from injuries.

Injury prevention. Walking subjects your body to approximately one-third the jarring that running does. Runners prone to overuse injuries should definitely give walking a try.

Style. Walking can improve running style, particularly posture, hip mobility, and smoothness of gait.

Ultramarathoning. Part of the strategy in the longer ultra-marathons is to hammer out some of the miles at a walk.

Racing. Race walking is a challenging and exciting event in its own right. Fifty-kilometer races are finished at a seven-minute-per-mile pace.

A walker always maintains contact with the earth; a runner does not. Keeping one foot on the ground at all times while propelling yourself forward can take the following forms.

Brisk Walking

Walking can provide the beginner or the runner coming back from an injury with all the workout needed. The beginner will find it easy to get the heart rate above 50 percent and can hold the pulse in the target range with simple variations of pace.

As long as you are walking, you should work on habits that will make you a better runner.

- Point your toes straight ahead. Whatever fatigue and soreness this costs you at first will be more than paid back when you begin running with correct footfalls.
- Hold your body erect. You should have a sense of stretching from your tailbone to the back of your head *but not to the point of creating tension.*
- Use a push with the back of the leg. Free your hips to swivel as you walk. This can help your running stride become more efficient.

Jog-Walk

Beginners in good shape and beginners who work up from brisk walking can try the jog-walk. It's purpose is to keep your heart rate in its proper exercise target range by speeding up to a jog when the rate dips and slowing to a walk when it soars.

For many fitness buffs, the jog-walk is their routine, year-in, year-out. And that's fine, particularly for those in their seventies and beyond. Beware, however, that you don't stay comfortable with jog-walking after it has ceased to do you good. Check your pulse every week during your jog-walk to

Bruce McDonald walking a 7:53.8 mile

make certain it is still strenuous enough to keep your heart rate in the target range.

The strategy for improving your fitness with the jog-walk is to start out with more walk than jog and progress to more jog than walk and ultimately to all jog. Divide a twenty-minute workout into four five-minute sections. Start by jogging a minute and a half out of each five minutes, then, as your heart rate indicates you are progressing, increase the amount of time spent jogging in each section by ten to thirty seconds.

Probably every one to five weeks you will increase the amount of time spent jogging. Keep that time fixed from workout to workout, and make adjustments for daily fluctuations in your energy level with pace. In other words, if you have progressed to three minutes of jogging in each five-minute section, you will maintain that from day to day until you increase it. On days when you're too pooped to pop, jog for the whole three minutes (unless real discomfort is caused) but at a reduced pace from your better workouts.

Exercise physiologists tout this jog-walk progression as the ideal routine for over-40 (sometimes over-35 or even over-30) beginners. Those who prefer to run unencumbered by watch and thoughts of time, can easily approximate this program but should use a watch in the beginning at least until they get a feel for the times and heart rates involved.

Here too, do not neglect thoughts of style. Avoid the plodding, heavy-footfall type of jog. Instead, use a gliding shuffle, keeping your feet low to the ground. As always, point your toes ahead, keep your back straight, and push off with your foot on each step.

Whether the jog portion of your jog-walk is more a run or a walk matters little to your heart. If you plan to work up to race walking, you might keep to more of a walking stride. If you plan to work up to running, you might lift your feet a little more and run.

Race Walking

Walking races date back to sixteenth-century Europe. True race walking began around the turn of the century, and races were popular, even as a spectator sport, both in the United States and Europe. Race walking was instated as an Olympic event in 1908 and in the early years was dominated by colorful characters. Interest in race walking started a decline in the Forties, and the event was dropped from Olympic competition after 1972.

Difficulties in judging race walking also contributed to its demise. A walker has to do two things:

1. Touch the advancing foot to the ground before lifting the rear foot (violation known as "lifting").

2. Straighten the knee of the supporting leg as it passes under the hips (violation is known as "creeping").

Nevertheless, there is mounting interest in race walking, and its adherents are confident it will even resume its place in the Olympics soon. Race walking is a skill that is tricky to master. If you want to take up the sport, you will do best to find a coach for occasional pointers or a running club with a race walking program (increasingly common). If you just want to try your legs at it, here are some guidelines.

Hip rotation

Hips. The hips must rotate, more so than is common in running (race walking loosens up the pelvic girdle—a big plus for older runners). As each leg swings forward, its hip reaches forward and down for maximum stride length.

Foot plant. Walkers move heel-to-toe. The heel is planted firmly into the ground, and a powerful pull starts. Competitive race walkers rely more on pull from the heel than push with the toes.

Good stride and arm motion

Knee lock. Almost as soon as the heel touches down, the knee of the supporting leg should lock hard to increase the pull of the leg. Remember, the leg must be straight as it passes beneath the body, but if you are walking correctly, your leg will be locked rather than merely straight.

Lift off. As soon as the knee of the supporting leg locks, the knee of the trailing leg should be thrust forward. This, more than anything else, determines the walker's speed.

Arms. Walkers use their arms for a powerful drive—upper body strength is a definite asset. The arms should be bent about 90 degrees and should swing so that the hand goes no further back than the hip joint. Arms held too high lead to lifting, held too low lead to a sluggish pace.

Trunk. The body should be upright. Leaning forward or tilting the head forward contributes to lifting. Swaying or leaning back leads to fatigue since energy must be expended for balancing the body.

As a further point, in race walking the feet will follow a single line as in running rather than parallel lines as in other types of walking. Runners will find this useful since any departure from true form (crossing the feet, spreading the feet, or turning the feet out) will be evidenced by lifting. Race walking can therefore be used to improve running gait.

Race walkers should strive for a sense of pulling the ground along beneath them. You'll know you have it when you feel a good turn in your hips and a toe lift just as the heel of the other foot lands. Once you get this movement synchronized, begin to work on speed of the trailing leg as it swings through for the next plant and on the swing of the arms to help power your stride.

Chapter 11

Jogging

The one thing that can be universally agreed on is that "jogging" implies a slower pace than "running" does. Otherwise, there is no agreement on what constitutes the difference between running and jogging.

Sprinters often suggest that running begins when you start landing on the ball of the foot—all else is jogging.

Physiologists try to make pace distinctions: running begins under a seven-minute-per-mile pace, or eight-minute, or nine-minute.

Others say that jogging occurs when you wear gray sweats and sneakers, running begins when you buy tricot shorts and waffle trainers.

For the purposes of this book, jogging refers simply to the slower ranges of running.

Chapter 12

Running

Do you consider yourself a jogger or a runner? The older you are, the more likely you refer to yourself as a jogger, and that's fine by the way. The only question becomes, have you avoided picking up the pace for fear of overexerting yourself? or because you think you are not capable of more speed? or maybe because you feel a faster pace is not appropriate for someone your age?

Just in case those concerns have been on your mind, we feel it worthwhile to tell you you have nothing to hold you back. Assuming you have been jogging for at least a few months now, you can pick up the pace without undue concern for these two reasons:

- The muscular action of the legs during running assists the circulation, reducing the strain on the heart. For this reason, if you perform an equivalent amount of work running and, say, shoveling snow, your heart will function 25 or 30 percent more efficiently during the running. The faster you run, the more circulatory assist you get.
- Muscles have two properties that assist the runner: elasticity and the stretch reflex. A stretched muscle automatically returns to its original length, and in the process, it performs "free" work. Elastic energy may account for as much as 50 percent of work performed efficiently. The stretch reflex is the property of muscles to rebound more

quickly the more quickly they are stretched. When moving at a slow jog, little advantage is taken of these properties; in fact, isometric contractions of opposing muscles will act to contain elastic force. Jogging can be more fatiguing than running.

What about injuries, you say? If you are running properly, not overpronating, not overstriding, not landing too heavily, you should experience no more injuries from running than jogging. Running offers all the benefits of jogging and more (the main one being that you get faster faster). So, why not run?

RUNNING

Sprinting at five strides a second as world-class track men do makes maximum use of muscle elasticity, the stretch reflex, and the pumping action of the leg muscles. However, the energy required to maintain such leg speed is enormous, plus lactic acid build-up during a sprint will eventually slow the runner. If you intend to run for more than fifteen seconds you will need to adjust the pace down from your maximum.

Running, then, is the activity that occupies the space between jogging and sprinting. Very roughly, running takes place from a five- to ten-minute-per-mile pace. At first, you may find a ten-minute-per-mile pace impossible for even two or three miles, but if you are moving near your limit with the aim of improving your time, who's to say you're not running?

Everyone can run (physical defects aside). That is, everyone moves their limbs in proper sequence to produce a running motion. No one needs to be taught to run, but advice can improve running ability.

THE KEY TO RUNNING

Perhaps the most important single factor in improving running ability is relaxation. This follows from the fact that most of your improvement will come from increased muscle coordination, not muscle speed or strength. If you settle into a comfortable pace, not tense, not forcing yourself, you allow

Running with a friend

the muscles and joints to accustom themselves to the movement. Over time, they—not you, (you won't even be conscious
of the particulars)—will learn to move much more efficiently.

Tension produces fatigue by itself and by creating tightness
that must be overcome. Learn to sense tension in your body
as you run, and experiment with ways to overcome it. Avoid

excessive motion of the legs, arms, trunk, or head as that will produce fatigue and maybe tension.

Think of yourself as gliding, running softly. Joe Henderson says "run gently," and there's no better advice. There will be times when you really want to push yourself, such as for strength training, but gentle running will always constitute the bulk of your running program.

Running, Head to Toe

The following checklist serves as a guide to reducing tension as you run. If you'll run through it mentally every half mile or so during your workout, you should be able to counteract bad tendencies from the start. Soon, you will settle into a natural running form and need to check yourself only every few runs.

Head. Strive for the sensation that your head is hooked on a static line and gliding straight forward through space. Don't let it tilt, wobble, or bob.

Eyes. Your eyes should scan the path ten to thirty yards ahead. As much as possible, use eye motion rather than head motion when you must look around.

Jaw. Soften your jaw. Use only enough energy to keep your teeth from knocking into each other. Gritted teeth are a very common source of tension.

Neck. Seek a slight sensation of stretch in the back of the neck. Back and shoulder soreness frequently results from looking upward with the resultant bow in the neck.

Shoulders. Do not hunch your shoulders. Also, your shoulders should move in synch with your hips; otherwise, you are twisting your torso unnecessarily.

Arms. Arms should move easily back and forth with the elbow cocked at about 90 degrees. Do not let your arms swing across midchest. Until you start sprinting, you will not need to pump with your arms.

Hands. Clenched hands are the most obvious sign of body tension. Run with your hands loosely cupped or with the thumbs lightly touching the fingertips.

Back. You want to run erect. Try for a sense of creating space between each vertebra, but don't make your back rigid.

Stomach. If you let your stomach muscles relax completely, your stomach will sag and you'll get a backache. Stretch your stomach until you feel a hollow sensation. Bent-leg sit-ups will help develop muscle tone so that you can relax the stomach muscles with confidence they will still do their job. Remember, you breathe with those muscles.

Hips. Your pelvis should ride squarely as you run. All too commonly the pelvis tilts forward. Counteract that by pushing the tailbone forward to bring the pelvis square again.

Legs. An economical, fluid stride is what it's all about. Cross-over in the gait, choppiness in the stride, woodenleggedness—all such traits detract from running efficiency.

Feet. A pair of excellent and well-fitting running shoes will offer your feet stability and allow them to relax. Make certain your foot is not striking the ground while still ahead of the knee, causing jarring and loss of speed.

Heels. Your foot should strike down just to the outside of the middle of the heel.

Toes. Toes should point ahead as you land on your heel and roll through to toe-off. Too much deviation either way can cause fatigue and soreness in the feet, ankles, and lower legs, eventually even in the hips or back. With the toes pointed ahead, the balls of the feet can bear your weight evenly. Pronation (toeing out) can be observed in your footprint in soft dirt. Also, as you come off your toe, spring forward, not upward—bouncing is a waste of speed and energy.

But the best monitor of your degree of relaxation will be your mind. Does running seem smooth and relatively effortless or does it seem heavy and forced? Do you notice tension or fatigue anywhere in your body as you run? Even more important, do you notice tension in your body *before* you run? In that case, you would do well to remember the advice from chapter 7 and relax for a few minutes before starting your warm-up.

THE COMPONENTS OF RUNNING

Running falls into the category known as repetitive work, the stringing together of a series of nearly identical motions, which includes such other activities as swimming, bicycling, and sawing. The two outstanding features of repetitive work are the essential motion and the cadence.

The Mechanical Components

In the case of running, stride is the essential motion and cadence is referred to as pace. With knowledge of a given runner's average stride length and leg speed, the distance covered can easily be computed if elapsed time is known, and vice versa.

So, all running boils down to these two components. Obviously the longer and faster the stride, the better the runner will perform.

Not quite the case. In fact, in a study of collegiate track men it was found that stride *shortened* an average of three inches as the runners improved over four years.

The foremost researcher into running stride is Dr. Peter Cavanagh of Penn State University. His early investigations of stride length (his subjects were elite runners) indicate:

1. There is no correlation between leg length and optimal stride length.
2. Your stride length will vary according to running speed and the gradient of the terrain.
3. Your optimal stride length for a given speed will develop subconsciously.
4. Your optimal stride length may change as you grow older.

Cavanagh has determined that stride length is a very individual thing. Everyone has a range within which length variation has little effect on efficiency, but that range cannot be predicted, only measured, so far. Furthermore, those who tend to run on the long side of their range find overstriding much more costly than understriding, while the opposite is true for those who run on the short side of their range.

What this boils down to is that in the absence of a biomechanist and laboratory, you will have to trust your body. You may be able to help your body adjust by experimenting

Running to the applause of the crowds

with different stride lengths occasionally and by trying uphill
and downhill running.

As you increase your pace from slow jog to fast sprint, your
stride length increases, and in doing so it counts much more
toward your overall speed than your increase in leg speed does.
In other words, faster running depends much more on increased
stride length than on faster leg movement. However, you also
know that you have an optimum stride length at a given pace

and that you cannot exceed a particular pace if you want to cover a particular distance in good fashion. It follows that for improving your speed over a particular distance, leg speed takes on more importance than stride length.

Leg speed is the frequency with which you complete strides. Overall speed is leg speed times stride length. A runner with a five-foot stride must take thirty-six more strides per minute to keep up with a runner making six-foot strides. For many, a compact stride affords greater leg speed; races do not necessarily go to the longest strider.

To increase leg speed you must look at two key areas, strength and efficiency. Both are improved by running, running, and more running. Weight training and, particularly, resistance running (see chapter 14) can improve leg strength dramatically. Speed-work will help develop fast-twitch muscle fibers, which on a diet of long slow distance may not get much of a workout.

Efficiency is a product both of good mechanical form and muscular coordination. And that brings us to the physical components of running.

The Physical Components

Any discussion of running mechanics becomes purely hypothetical in the absence of a particular runner. The legs can maintain their stride and pace only as long as the heart, lungs,, and muscles hold out. The physical limits are these:

- aerobic capacity
- muscular endurance
- muscular strength
- skill
- flexibility

Except for flexibility, all these components are best improved by running.

Aerobic Capacity. Aerobic capacity is the sum of the efficiency of the lungs, heart, vessels, and oxidative reactions of the muscles. Long-distance running will raise aerobic capacity to its maximum. This is such an important component that it is possible to predict marathon results with fair accuracy by ranking the runners according to their maximum aerobic capacity. However, such notable runners as Frank Shorter and Derek Clayton have not had exceptional aerobic capacities and have succeeded through skill and efficiency.

Muscular Endurance. The muscles work by virtue of their ability to oxidize glucose and fats. Glucose is a short-term fuel, fat a limitless fuel (even the 5 percent body fat of world-class runners is more than sufficient). Until you have put in several long-distance runs, your body will not become an efficient fat-burner. Running long distances increases the number, size, and enzyme content of the mitochondria, the agents within the muscle responsible for oxidizing the fuel, and thereby postpones the "hitting the wall" that occurs when glycogen stores have been depleted.

Obviously, muscular endurance increases as aerobic capacity increases. However, muscular endurance is much more activity-specific. That is, if you train as a runner then try bicycling or swimming, your muscular endurance is much more likely to give out before your aerobic endurance.

Muscular Strength. Strength is simply the ability to supply enough force to move a weight (in this case, your body). You may have more than enough strength for your usual running, but how much does your pace fall off when you start uphill?

With increased muscle power, you can move your legs faster as has already been mentioned, and you won't experience such a great drop-off as you move up a grade. Interestingly, by increasing your muscular strength, you decrease the likelihood of experiencing the heavy legs common with running long slow distance exclusively.

Skill. Skill is something of a catch-all term. As already mentioned, everyone is capable of moving limbs in such a fashion as to produce a run. Skill comes not from the sequence of bodily events so much as from the timing and direction of the events.

About 7 percent of a runner's improvement over the first couple of years will be owing to improvements in running efficiency—skill, in other words. This includes decreases in the amount of resistance opposing muscles may offer, synchronizing upper and lower body movements, grooving stride length, and making the most of mechanical advantages.

Running alone

In another sense, skill refers to a runner's savvy, the amount of experience the runner can draw on. Very often, the race goes to the runner who knows how much of a kick he or she has left or who knows how closely to keep up with a fast initial pace and so on.

Flexibility. Flexibility refers not only to the joints—obviously, a door with well-oiled hinges moves more easily than one with rusty hinges—but also to muscle viscosity. Warming up the muscles reduces their natural resistance to stretching and increases their oxygen content. Bodily tension also increases muscular resistance. Remember to relax.

Each of these components has been the subject of numerous articles, even entire books. Who would think so much could be said about something that is nothing more than the rapid repetition of long steps?

Running is a simple activity which will challenge you for a lifetime, whether you already have been running for forty years or are just beginning. To make the most of the challenge, consider yourself a laboratory. Relax and tune in to the feedback of your apparatus. Experiment, discuss, read, refine, adjust. You'll stay amazed that way.

Chapter 13

Sprinting

Most masters runners have little interest in sprinting. Their view runs like this: "Training is putting money in the bank; sprinting depletes my savings." Other masters runners thrive on sprinting, and the popularity of sprinting in masters track is showing decided increases.

There is good reason to be cautious about sprinting. Sprinting takes muscles, tendons, heart, and lungs to their limit. Injuries lie in wait of the first time you neglect your warm-up, stretch your stride too far, or run when exhausted.

For those who run pain-free there is much to be said in favor of sprinting.

1. Sprinting increases the power and speed of the legs. The quadriceps, ankles, and fast-twitch muscle fibers are exercised much more than in running.
2. Sprinting increases heart-stroke volume. While distance runners outshine sprinters in overall cardiovascular fitness, sprinting does increase the size and power of the heart muscle.
3. Sprinting produces anaerobic fitness by increasing the body's tolerance of lactic and pyruvic acids, by raising the exercise level at which these acid wastes are produced, by improving the body's ability to metabolize high-energy phosphates, and also by improving the body's ability to recover from oxygen debt.

The popularity of distance events among masters runners has often been attributed to the fact that speed abandons the body at a greater rate than endurance does. However, the evidence compiled by Ken Young at the National Running Data Center in Tucson, Arizona, shows this isn't so.

The chart below will make this clear.

Age	Percent Decline 100 Meters	Percent Decline Marathon
35	4.7	1.3
40	8.1	4.5
45	11.8	9.0
50	16.0	14.5
55	22.0	20.9
60	28.6	27.5
65	35.9	34.8
70	43.2	42.5
75	50.8	50.3
80	58.5	58.1

When you consider that the performance decline in the sprint event is based on an optimum age of 23 versus 29 for the marathon, you can see there is very little difference. Furthermore, as a larger and better-trained pool of masters runners enter the sprints, the discrepancy should disappear.

Are You a Sprinter?

The swelling tide of masters sprinters comprises mostly ex-sprinters who turned coach and are now returning to racing. Payton Jordan (see page 123 for his profile) typifies such a background. On the other hand, newcomers to running are more frequently turning their attention to sprints. Harry Koppel typifies this class of sprinter.

Harry took up swimming to help recuperate from treatment of throat cancer (an occupational hazard for a chemist) in 1974 at the age of 60. Soon, he held age-group records for the 50 and 100 meter breast stroke. The calamities had not stopped, however. In February 1976, Harry was swimming in a sleepy Hawaiian lagoon where he trespassed on a highly poisonous sea

All out in a 100-yard dash

snake. The bite caused severe atrophy in his leg, and Harry took up jogging to combat the wasting of his muscles.

Soon he was training on a steady diet of pace intervals, running fifteen 100 meter dashes, six 200 meter sprints, or four 400 meter sprints for his workout. In May 1978, he put his training to the test in an exhibition run led by Olympian Eddie Hart at San Mateo College in California. He finished in 11.8 seconds, a world record for age 64.

What type of runner is, like Harry Koppel, drawn directly to sprints? Probably the main determining factor is the proportion of red slow-twitch muscle fibers (endurance) to white fast-twitch fibers (speed). The more fast-twitch, the greater the speed of the muscles. The ratio of the two types of fibers is genetically determined and is not alterable.

It is possible to determine the exact ratio of fast- to slow-twitch fibers with a muscle biopsy. However, few labs perform this test; it's expensive; and it's not painless. If you don't find yourself naturally drawn to a personal best event, you can try the vertical jump test. If your flatfooted jump exceeds 30 inches, you're definitely a sprinter, less than 20 inches indicates a distance runner, and in-between measurements point to the middle distances as your best event.

Sprint Training

Regardless of your outcome in the vertical jump test, sprinting is worth a try if only to increase leg speed and lactic-acid tolerance for your preferred distance event.

- Sprinting up a gradual slope yields the best results in leg strength and speed.
- Sprinting down a gradual slope is the best method of increasing stride length. Watch out for injuries, though.
- Sprint intervals of less than fifteen seconds followed by two to three minutes of recovery build leg speed in an acid-free state.
- Sprint intervals of 200 meters and more increase anaerobic thresholds.

Distance runners can include sprints in fartlek (see next chapter) or may do sprint intervals every week or ten days as a workout variant. With aerobic capacities leveling out, resulting in much more even competition in distance racing, success is depending more and more on the kick at the end of the race. That is where sprint workouts are particularly helpful.

Sprinting differs from running in four main ways:

1. The knees lift much higher.
2. The arms work much harder.
3. The stride is longer.
4. The toe lands before the heel (In short sprints, the heel doesn't touch down).

To learn sprinting, run in place on the balls of your feet with waist-high knee movement (hold your hands out at waist level to make sure). Learn to relax while doing this.

Once you feel comfortable moving down the track in the fashion mentioned above, add foreleg reach. To further increase your stride length, land on the ball of your foot, lower the foot flat as you pass over, then toe off. (Try running stiff-legged to strengthen your ankle "flip.")

Next, add arm power. Let your arms hang to your side, raise the forearms to 90 degrees, cup your fingers into a loose fist, and, as you sprint, pump your arms hard to increase the speed of your legs.

The key to sprinting is running upright and relaxed. Do not lean forward—stay tall. Also, propel yourself smoothly down-field—don't bounce. Concentrate on each step carrying you forward, not up and down.

Sprinting is an art that must be continually learned. Seek feedback on your style from experienced runners. Analyze one component of your sprint at a time at slower speed periodically, work on it, then groove it back into your sprint at increasingly fast speed.

Sprinting is constant challenge and exhilaration—a race to shave mere eyeblinks off your best time. If you have not tried sprinting for fear it would be too taxing, you owe yourself a crack at all-out running.

Chapter 14

Advanced Training

After the base is established, the principle of diminishing returns is usually in full effect. Making improvements in speed demands more and more effort. And the principle of specificity asserts itself to say that if you spend your time running moderate distances at moderate speeds, you'll be good at running moderate distances at moderate speeds.

Varying your workouts keeps your legs fresher, gives you a wider range of efficient muscle movement, lessens the chance of your getting bored, and improves your speed.

The important caution is to use these training techniques after you have established a base. Your base is your point of departure—you will run a percentage faster or slower or longer or shorter than your base. Another bit of caution is to start into each of these techniques gradually; your muscles will not function particularly efficiently at these tasks in the beginning and will thus be prone to soreness.

Various combinations of these techniques are used for the various running events. Every runner develops preferences for the methods of training for particular events, and every coach has an opinion as to the best mixture of methods for a given event. For instance, a 100-meter sprinter might train entirely on short sprint intervals while a marathon runner might rely solely on long slow distance. On the other hand, some marathoners have trained primarily on fast miles while some milers have trained on slow distance. Opinions vary so much that this chapter will serve as nothing more than a sampler. With the principle of individuality in mind, you should work out your own system anyway.

SLOW DISTANCE

Slow distance is the training method that helped you establish your base, and it will likely continue to be your most important training method. The idea behind slow distance is to get in enough running to stimulate a high degree of adaptation but to do so at such a pace that the runner is not hampered by exhaustion.

Slow distance was first formalized by Ernst van Aaken as the "Waldniel Pure-Endurance Method." He wrote, "Since the year 1928 when I watched Paavo Nurmi at the Amsterdam Olympics warm up for two hours before a race, it has been clear to me that modern civilized man is not lacking in speed but in endurance. This one thing, then, is necessary for all runners—to acquire the quality of endurance at the outset and then fight daily to keep it."

In the United States, Tom Osler gave this form of training the title "Base Training," and Joe Henderson gave it its most popular name: "Long Slow Distance" (LSD).

For van Aaken, slow distance is running that brings the heart rate only up to 130 beats a minute. Henderson says it is running comfortably—usually at about 80 percent of maximum for a given distance, or about a minute a mile slower than all-out.

You may ask why slow distance is considered a training method at all—isn't it just running easily and what's so special about that? For most runners slow distance is not a training method; it is simply the type of running they enjoy and derive their benefit from. Slow distance becomes a training method when it takes on a purpose within an individual's running goals. Again, that purpose is maintaining the mileage necessary for stamina and adaptation without facing burn-out.

The criticism of slow distance is that it does not promote specificity. That is, slow-distance runners do not experience race speeds and stresses. For those who run only for fun and fitness, that criticism is no cause for concern. For those who want to gradually improve their speed, occasional spurts of speed during a long, slow run will help. For those who take their running seriously, there are the training methods that follow.

FAST DISTANCE

Fast distance developed from the idea that slow distance may be all right for those whose interest in running is as a life-long activity but it certainly is not efficient use of a top athlete's peak years.

Its main proponents were Australians and New Zealanders: Arthur Lydiard, Ron Clarke, Peter Snell, Derek Clayton, and others during the early Sixties.

Basically, fast distance is running at 95 percent of race speed. The pace should be fast, yet controlled and relaxed. "Relaxed" is a key word here; by backing off slightly from race pace, many runners learn to be more comfortable with speed.

As an all-around training method, fast distance takes too much of a toll in exhaustion and injuries to suit any but the most Spartan runners. Its most prevalent use is as an occasional way to "top off" a training program before a particular race. For instance, marathoners often put in a "hard twenty" two weeks prior to a race. Such a strategy is thought to consolidate under racelike conditions all the training effort that went before while allowing ample time for recovery and further honing before the competition.

FARTLEK

Slow and fast distance are the two "steady-running" training methods. Other methods, lumped under the heading "intervals" (following), involve interrupting the running with periods of recovery. Fartlek, Swedish for "speed play," is the bastard child of both types of methods.

Fartlek is best looked at as an expression of the joy of running: accelerate, jog, bound, charge up hills, leap, walk. It is

Fell running

through such variety in pace and effort that fartlek produces leg
strength and raises aerobic and anaerobic thresholds.

A Swede named Gosta Holmer is credited with developing
the fartlek style in the Thirties as a way of taking advantage of
Scandinavian forest paths. Billy Squires, one of the United
States' most successful track coaches, offers this perspective:
"This system of fartlek is hard to explain, for it is less a formula

for training and competing than an expression of a strange breed of athletic artists. Maybe if one could understand it, though, one could appreciate its power—a power that sent Gunder Hagg and Arne Andersson through to mile records that stood unbeaten and unmatched for twenty years."

Fartlek appeals strongly to a self-contained, spontaneous type of runner, one who is alert to signals from the body. Many insist that fartlek, because it offers expression of spontaneity and creativity, allows them to get in more work before succumbing to fatigue. Certainly, most runners, given a choice of only one training method, would select fartlek for its flexibility and because it develops both speed and endurance, both aerobic and anaerobic capacity.

Other runners find fartlek not exacting enough, not capable of forcing them to reach their goals. That is why we point out that it appeals to "self-contained" runners. Those who need the constant prodding of stopwatches and known distances would do better to turn to intervals. However, runners who find themselves getting compulsive about improving their times would do well to engage only in fartlek until they get over their compulsion.

Some runners go in for what might be called "super fartlek," concentrating not so much on improving running speed as on building all-around leg strength and co-ordination. In this type of fartlek, participants indulge in leaping, skipping, backpeddling, carioca (running sideways by crossing legs back and forth), and all manner of strange methods for propelling the body over field and trail.

INTERVALS

Interval training is the product of scientists, the first result of laboratory testing being applied to running technique. The method was formalized in the Thirties by two German doctors: Woldemar Gerschler, a physiologist and coach, and Hans Reindell, a cardiologist. They relied on precise timing and distances, controlled recovery phases as measured by heart-rate recovery, and work loads expressed in formulas like 20 x 100 meters.

In 1939, Rudolf Harbig, a student of Gerschler, knocked two

seconds from the world 800-meter record, a mark which stood for sixteen years. Following the war, such eastern European stars as Emil Zatopek, Mihaly Igloi's students, Vladimir Kuts, and Pyotr Bolotnikov used interval training to great effect.

While interval training took a backseat to endurance running in the Sixties, it re-emerged in the Seventies. With their laboratory-on-an-oval-track atmosphere, intervals continue as the stepchild of scientists. Meanwhile, increased scientific understanding of running has shown that intervals are indeed the best method of increasing speed.

Intervals are endlessly adaptable. That is because they have five components:

- The distance covered in the run.
- The speed at which the distance is covered.
- The number of times the run is repeated.
- The length of the recovery between runs.
- The activity during the intervals.

For instance, a runner might select 10 (number of repetitions) times 440 (distance) at 61 seconds (speed) with 90 seconds (length of interval) jogging (activity) recoveries. Or 20 x 100 meters at 80 percent (speed) with recovery period determined by pulse rate during a walk.

It is good to keep in mind the Gerschler-Reindell law: "The running effort in interval training should send the heart rate to around 180 beats per minute. From this point, the heart is allowed 90 seconds to return to 120 to 125 beats per minute. If it takes longer, the effort demanded has either been too violent or too long." Older runners should revise the heart rates above in accordance with their ages.

As you might suspect, there is some disagreement as to what the best distances, speeds, intervals, and so forth are in training for given events. Here are some of the popular types of intervals:

Sprint intervals. Numerous repetitions of 40- to 50-meter runs at full speed with jogging recoveries have been shown to give excellent results for the 100- and 400-meter events.

Long sprints. Running repetitions of sprints at full speed over 200 to 600 meters to the point that the heart rate does not recover in a reasonable time is a good practice for the 400-meter event.

Endurance intervals. Relatively long runs at 60 to 80 percent speed with brief recovery periods help build endurance.

Surging. Surging is long slow distance with a surge to full speed thrown in periodically.

Pace intervals. Runs of race distance at 80 to 90 percent of race speed with long recoveries of 1½ to 3 minutes are one of the most popular ways of preparing for the 400- and 800-meter events.

It is possible to get in speedwork in a virtually acid-free state by keeping runs less than 100 meters long and intervals at least 30 seconds long. This can be continued over long periods of time. The body begins to produce lactic acid after about 15 seconds of hard activity, and the acid accumulation can bring the body to a stop within 20 seconds if the pace is not adjusted. By keeping the full-speed runs to less than a 15 second duration, the acid mechanism can be cheated. On the other hand, it is worthwhile also to use longer runs in order to improve the body's ability to work in an acid state.

RESISTANCE RUNNING

Why would you purposely set obstacles for yourself? Why run uphill if there is a level stretch nearby? Why carry weights when running? Is this part of the school of thought that advises you to hit yourself with a hammer because it'll feel good to stop?

No. Resistance running springs from the idea that if training is murder, races will be a relative breeze. This is the concept of overtraining, of becoming stronger than need be for a given event.

The common types of resistance running—hill running, sand running, running with weights, and bounding—have the common benefit of increasing leg strength and endurance. They are unsurpassed at accomplishing that end.

Several studies have pointed to uphill intervals as producing the most dramatic improvement in running speed. Fell running (so named for the fells, or hilly regions of England) is cross-country work over a rolling terrain. Distance runners find it helpful for leg speed and endurance as well as for developing uphill and downhill strides.

Those who have access to a beach may enjoy running in the sand—or even in the surf. Wearing strap-on ankle weights is more popular in Europe than in the States. Competitive runners feel that stride length may be more affected from weights than from other resistance methods.

Bounding, running with great, lifting strides, produces the same strengthening in the quadriceps and other leg muscles and should be considered a sort of self-imposed resistance. Bounding can easily be included in your fartlek.

Resistance running benefits both sprinters and distance runners. Distance runners build quadricep strength and endurance so vital to hanging in on the final miles. Sprinters gain improved stride and leg speed. However, attention should be paid to the fact that your stride against resistance will differ from your race stride. For that reason, resistance running should be used in proportion to other training techniques.

CIRCUIT TRAINING

Indoor and outdoor fitness circuits have long enjoyed popularity on the Continent and are starting a pronounced upswing in popularity here in the United States.

Indoor circuits are a blessing in areas that suffer foul winter weather. Commonly, these circuits offer a series of weight-lifting and exercise stations which must be completed against a time standard. If the area is large enough, participants may run between stations.

Some indoor circuits may be blessed with Universal or even Nautilus weight machines. Usually, however, free weights make up the lifting equipment. Rope climbs, chin ups, push ups, and sit ups are typical of the exercises included. The drawback is crowding of the facility on miserable days.

The most common outdoor circuit in the States is the Parcourse Fitness Circuit, which was patterned after the Vita Life circuits of Europe. Eighteen (sometimes nine) exercise and stretching stations are spread over a course averaging about two miles. Each station has three par values; so, for instance, at the sit-up station, starting par will be 5, sporting par 10, and championship par 15 completed sit ups.

Because the Parcourse system includes stretching stations, walking between some of the stations, and close monitoring of pulse rate, it is not designed to be run against time. These features do, however, recommend Parcourse circuits highly for use by older runners, who may find it offers everything needed for a total fitness program, particularly strenuous workouts for the whole body and objective feedback on progress.

Parcourse circuits can be found in virtually every major metropolitan area, especially on the West Coast. Also many industries offer such circuits on the premises. For further information, contact.

Parcourse, Ltd.
3701 Buchanan Street
San Francisco, California 94123

With or without running integrated into the circuit, circuit training should offer a complete cardiovascular workout. Runners will appreciate the opportunity to strengthen the upper body. So far, circuit training has been associated with weekend fitness buffs, but with world-class runners such as Sebastian Coe proclaiming its benefits, more and more serious runners are giving it a try.

If you are just beginning as a runner, it would be unfair to yourself to get too turned on or turned off by the advanced training methods discussed. If you're not interested, okay. You may find a year or two down the road that these forms of training offer just the challenge you need *at that point*. So don't prejudice yourself against them now.

By the same token, don't let yourself get too attracted to these training methods. They will offer much more satisfaction if you attempt them after establishing your base fitness level with about a year of running. (The exception here would be the Parcourse circuits, which many find a complete and satisfactory form of workout.) You may want to try these methods on occasion, but don't burn yourself out by training too heavily until you've established a strong base.

Chapter 15

Injuries

If you become a serious runner, you are going to hurt—no way around that. Veteran runners are accustomed to running with pain and use the term "injury" to mean only pains of sufficient magnitude to interrupt training. Pain is a particular problem for beginners, both because they encounter more of it and because they know less about it. Is that ice-pick-like pain in the knee going to vanish forever a mile down the road or is it a symptom of damage that will bring a running career to a halt before it gets a good start?

Roughly, injuries can be grouped under three headings: traumatic, environmental, and overuse. There is a special fourth category we will examine, which we will label "injury-prone physique."

TRAUMATIC INJURIES

The category of traumatic injury is simple to deal with in writing, not so in actuality. In general, if it is split, torn, bleeding, ruptured, sprained, broken, or aching more than you can deal with, see a *sports* podiatrist or physician for diagnosis and treatment.

Shame on you if you elevate simple overuse pains into this category. If a pain continues to hamper you or increases in severity from workout to workout, treat it with respect. Have it checked before you force something to give out.

114

OVERUSE INJURIES

Most pains, if treated with respect, have no lasting conse-
quences. Those leery of taking up running because of the
inevitability of pain, need not worry. Once experienced, the
great majority of the pain caused by running is viewable as a
nuisance. And, as more is learned about the cause of running
pains, pain becomes even less of a factor.

Four things will prevent virtually all injuries: proper shoes,
stretching, avoidance of strain, and body awareness.

Shoes

Any problem inflicted by your footwear inflicts itself eight
hundred times to the mile times the number of miles you run.
*Do not take your first running step until you have acquired
properly fitting running shoes!* Do not run in sneakers, Hush
Puppies, or bare feet. Do not buy the $15 wonders in discount
markets. Buy a top-brand running shoe.

By this point, the deviations in quality among the top brands
are minimal. The best consumer advice is (1) Read the *Runner's
World* shoe issue each October for the latest information on
available shoe models. (2) Go to a specialty sport shoe store
with sales clerks who run. Ask for their advice. (3) Of the shoes
with the features you want, buy the pair that fits best.
(4) Don't hesitate to scrap a pair of new $35 shoes if they don't
work right for you. In fact, more runners are seeing the wisdom
in owning several models of shoes to minimize the influence of
a particular brand. (5) Don't run on shoes that have worn out.
(6) If you are not a C width, shop for brands that offer your
width. The angles and fits of the various running shoes are
worked out within surprisingly narrow tolerances. Wear, particularly uneven wear, can turn a good shoe into a bad one. By
the way, consult your podiatrist if your shoes show unusual
wear patterns, and take your shoes with you whenever you
visit your podiatrist.

Hint: The first ten or twenty times you put on a new pair of
shoes, lace them all the way to make certain the fabric adjusts
to give you a good fit.

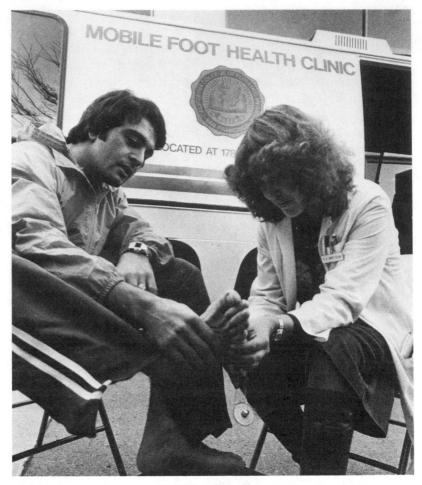

A house call

Stretching

Stretching reduces the amount of nuisance pain while also raising the threshold at which muscle tissue can be damaged by excessive forces. Omitting stretching exercises is not wise (see chapter 9).

Avoiding Strain

The beginning running program in chapter 8 of this book is based on a six-week adjustment period, a period in which the body will gradually accustom itself to increasing levels of activity. The greatest key to pain-free running lies in never overdoing it. Don't make sizable increases in distance or pace beyond your *recent* training levels.

Be aware that you don't have to feel the strain for it to be there. Runners are frequently lured into more miles than planned when overcome by the sensation of fluid, effortless stride, and they usually pay for that indiscretion with pain and reduced mileage for the following week or two.

Pace and distance are not the only sources of strain. Flaws in style, such as overstriding or bounding, increase strain on muscles and joints. Extremes in temperature tax the body as can diet and frame of mind. Consider all sources and adjust your training accordingly.

Body Awareness

If you can tune in to the strain your body is experiencing and act accordingly, you can eliminate much grief. Most injuries don't just happen—there is a buildup period. If you are sensitive to the signals, you can usually catch injuries before they happen.

The most obvious signals include:

- tiredness from the previous day's run
- mild stiffness or soreness (in conditioned runners; beginners can expect mild aches)
- swollen lymph glands
- nervousness, sleeplessness, or irritability
- stomach pains, loss of appetite coupled with loss of weight
- fever blisters, sniffles, headache, and other symptoms of reduced resistance
- stumble-footedness and lead-leggedness
- nagging fatigue and general sluggishness

When such signals appear, slack off on your mileage and pace until the spring returns to your legs. You probably just saved yourself an injury.

Treatment

Most overuse injuries manifest themselves as inflammation. The rule is cold for new injuries, heat for old. Aspirin helps too.

If, for instance, you develop a chronically sore knee, ice it for several minutes after each run and take as many as four aspirin (along with bland food or drink to offset stomach irritation). Use a heating pad or hot soak before running and at whatever other times that may seem helpful.

ENVIRONMENTAL INJURIES

Heat can kill you. Fortunately, over-40 runners are not frequently victims of heat since the antidote is prudence. When faced with the prospect of running in temperatures above 70 degrees, work to build up your heat resistance. (1) Reduce your pace and mileage building them up again over a three-week period. (2) Drink one glass of water every twenty minutes when running in hot weather. (3) Shade your head and douse it with water now and then. (4) Run in the shade.

Electrolyte-replacement drinks, such as Body Punch and Gatorade, can be valuable during the three weeks you spend adjusting to hot weather, particularly if you are out of condition to start with.

If you are training in a cool climate for a hot-weather run elsewhere, running in sweats or warm-ups will give you the same effect as running in atmospheric heat.

Over-40 runners are frequently overly cautious about cold weather. Shorts and T-shirt, once you've warmed up, are adequate for temperatures down to 40 degrees. Below 40 you can add sweats, jackets, mufflers, mittens, and so on to stave off the chill, but you need not do it to the extent most older runners seem to think necessary.

What you do need to be aware of in temperatures below 40 degrees, no matter how well bundled you are, is your breathing. Drawing cold air into the lungs can chill the bronchial tubes triggering a nerve response that constricts the tubes and makes breathing difficult. Counteract this by wearing a scarf or surgical mask in chilly weather and a muffler or ski mask in really cold weather.

Running in sub-zero weather is no problem if you dress properly, but do keep alert to wind-chill. Hypothermia (loss of body heat) can kill, and it slips up on its victim without warning. Unless you get stranded or take a really long run, you are in little danger of hypothermia as you will be generating plenty of heat (in another sense you are depleting body heat— so don't stay out long after your run).

Inhaling auto exhaust is another form of environmental injury. The worst apparent effects are shortness of breath, dizziness, and headache—no real injury, but avoid exhaust and pollution nevertheless. Foods, additives, and pollens are another form of environmental problem for many. Dr. Joan Ullyot states that feelings of faintness accompanied by heart irregularity and sweating are most likely caused by allergy to some food or by monosodium glutamate, not by running.

INJURY-PRONE PHYSIQUE

A tendency to running injuries is inherent in some people's makeup. The five leading conditions that predispose to injury are:

1. *Morton's foot.* Morton's foot, the presence of a long second toe, leads to hammer toe and weakens arches. Similarly, a long big toe leads to bunions. If you have either condition, see a podiatrist before running.

2. *Splayed feet.* Those with feet that point outward while running are heir to spasms, corns, and excessive soreness. Furthermore, regular running shoes only exaggerate the problem. See a podiatrist.

3. *Leg-length discrepency.* Most hip pain is caused by one leg being shorter than the other (or by running on a cambered surface, which can produce the same effect). The solution lies in placing a felt pad in the shoe of the shorter leg.

4. *Obesity.* Excess weight adds to the jarring the joints take with each footstrike. Many types of injuries are common to overweight runners.

5. *Arch problems.* Watch out if you have high arches (cavus foot) or low arches (flat feet). See a podiatrist before running.

If you find yourself prone to injuries during the early weeks of running, split your training between running and some other aerobic activity, such as cycling, swimming, or rowing, that places less stress on the legs. Meanwhile, consult your podiatrist or orthopedist.

It is possible to go into the subject of injuries in much greater depth. There is not one word here about stress fractures, shin splints, stitches, or other common runner's afflictions. Such conditions are covered much more thoroughly in books such as Dr. Steven Subotnick's *Cures for Common Running Injuries,* and *Dr. George Sheehan's Medical Advice for Runners.*

One last piece of advice, however, on injuries: never use an injury as an excuse. There is a tendency, surprisingly strong in some individuals, to rationalize poor performance by dramatizing some minor ailment that probably would never have been noticed otherwise. More often than seems possible, injuries that originate in the head appear in the body. If you are hurt, ease up. If you are running poorly, you are running poorly. If you are losing a race, you are losing a race. Don't succumb to the temptation to use an injury as a scapegoat.

Part Three

Profiles

Profiles

The brief biographical sketches that follow can do no more than acquaint you with a very few of the many people who typify masters running. In the last five years, running has become the most popular outlet for Americans over 40, and masters running has become the most creative and vital form of running, eclipsing collegiate, even Olympic, competition in its contribution to enhancing public opinion of the sport.

All the runners who are fun to read about are older than 40. Those with flavor, character, wit, and verve are beyond 40. Those with dedication, stick-to-it-iveness, and guts have passed 40. Those who are "over the hill" are the only ones picking up speed. With this in mind, we apologize for not offering more profiles and for not giving more detail in the ones that follow.

Payton Jordan

Destiny—a resistless, inescapable force that predetermines the course of life—perhaps you say. But whether it was fate or just a natural partnership, Payton Jordan has spent the vast majority of his very successful career on or near a track.

The path of this career was set into motion early, when as a young boy living in Southern California he attended the 1932 Olympic Games. He recalls telling his mother that he too would someday compete on a track.

By age 17 his prophesy was already reality. He set junior college records with a 9.6 in the 100-yard dash and a 21.1 in the

200. His 21.1 qualified him for the 1936 Olympic Trials. He finished fourth, just missing a berth on the American team.

Though World War II canceled the Olympics of 1940 and 1944, sports writers indulged in some imaginary casting. Jordan was named on their sprint team for both the 100- and 200-meter dashes.

By the time the war had ended Jordan passed his athletic peak, made the transition from athlete to coach. First at Occidental College and now at Stanford University, Jordan continues his successful track career. In 1968 his coaching prowess was publicly acknowledged when he was named head coach of the U.S. Olympic track-and-field team. Jordan's team, one of the strongest ever fielded by the United States, brought home twenty-four medals, twelve of them gold.

Four years later friends persuaded him to resume running after nearly thirty years on the sidelines. Those friends must have known that Jordan still had ample ability—since his return to running in 1972, he has set twenty-two masters marks in distances from the 50-yard dash to the 220.

Adhering to the technique he has taught over the years, Jordan really practices what he preaches. "I work very hard one day and light the next. I don't like to do the masochistic training. But when I work, I work like the devil." He averages forty minutes of running a day, following coaching his team's practice.

Jordan continues to run for the joy of it, "I've always gotten tremendous thrills out of participation. I enjoy it as much now as I did when I was a kid."

Miki Gorman

If you are a mother with a new baby, you are busy. In between changing diapers, answering cries, feeding, bathing, and the myriad of baby-related callings, there is time for little else—for most women. Miki Gorman made the time for running.

In 1976 with her daughter Danielle still crawling, Gorman continued training and was in top shape. She was training for the fabled New York City Marathon.

At the age of 41 she ran a 2:39:11 marathon, setting a

Miki Gorman (No. 4)

master's record that still stands. She had improved her personal record by more than seven minutes.

With her goal of running a sub 2:40 marathon accomplished, Miki felt somewhat lost. "After 1976, my motivation wasn't high because I didn't know what to shoot for," she reflects. She added that her view of running also began to change at that time. "Before my 2:39, I wanted to win and break my personal record. Now I'm not as interested in high quality training. Also, Danielle needs more attention. I average about seventy miles a week. Some weeks my mileage gets much higher and, of course, some weeks it's lower."

Casual as her new approach to training may be, Gorman has continued to win competitions. She came home from the 1977 World Masters Track-and-Field Championships in Sweden with four gold medals.

Although her time of 2:57:08 was far from Gorman's best, in 1978 she again was the top masters woman finisher in the New York Marathon. Since then, promotional work with Avon has consumed a major portion of her time. She has four trips to

Japan scheduled for 1979 to organize road races for Japanese women.

Gorman continues to be enthusiastic about the concept of masters running, "I want masters competition to be active and thrive. I don't want to see runners quitting."

Despite multiple outside interests and obligations, Gorman has no intention of being a quitter. She plans to run again in the 1979 masters championships, and she thinks she could still run a 2:36 marathon "if I start training hard."

Jimmy Carter

There are as many different reasons to run as there are occupations of runners. True, some run because everyone else does, others for fitness, and many to lose weight. But a man who ought to know has found running to be a natural tranquilizer, a means to release some of the pressure of one of the world's most intense jobs, and a quiet time spent alone to weigh thoughts and sort ideas. The man—Jimmy Carter; his occupation—President.

Actually, for the President, this is more appropriately termed a return to running. As a plebe (freshman) at the U.S. Naval Academy, some thirty-five years ago, he earned his numeral running for the cross-country team.

Mr. Carter's physician, Dr. William Lukash, approves of his running. Following an examination the doctor saw no reason why he shouldn't begin, "The President was in excellent shape, and he simply started running."

He averages five miles a day, keeping a brisk eight-minute-per-mile pace. Dr. Lukash reports that the president's pulse is down to a low 45.

Such a slow pulse did not surprise the doctor. He related that Jimmy Carter observes a strict fitness regimen. During the summer he plays tennis and softball, avoids elevators in favor of stairs, and generally involves himself in physical activity as much as possible.

Mr. Carter begins his runs before dinner between 4:30 and 6:30 p.m. He takes one of two quarter-mile routes; one by the North Portico of the White House, the other on the South Lawn's oval driveway. Both are paved, on Dr. Lukash's advice, though the President prefers grass. Lukash feels that it is "much safer to jog on the pavement."

On occasion, members of the White House staff are surprised to see First Lady Rosalyn accompany her husband for several laps. Lukash commented that the President enjoys having the occasional company.

Ellery Clark, Jr., Jimmy Carter's cross-country coach at Annapolis speculated on why the President originally opted for running; "I assume, due to his light build and his interest in running for fun, he didn't give soccer or football any particular thought." Clark remembers Mr. Carter's now famous grin. "Cross-country practice was the only time he flashed it. He used to relax and enjoy his practice without the pressures of being a plebe under the close eye of the upperclassmen."

For President Jimmy Carter running has proven to be more than just a fad—it allows him momentary escape from the close eye of the world.

Raymond Fowler

You might expect great things from someone who takes up running to get back in shape and twelve months later has qualified for and run in the Boston Marathon. Indeed, Raymond Fowler, a professor of psychology at the University of Alabama, has some outstanding accomplishments to point to.

In the three years since he began running at age 46, he has won several races from two-milers to the marathon and founded the Association of Running Psychologists. He has a personal record of 3:12 in the marathon, and the club he founded has quickly become the largest of its kind. More than one thousand psychologists took part in the run Dr. Fowler organized for the 1979 meeting of the American Psychological Association.

Walt Stack

Walt Stack, most commonly referred to as "the amazing Walt Stack," has a workout that would leave most runners cold. Weekdays, starting in the wee morning hours through chill San Francisco air, Walt runs seventeen miles. This is followed by a

Walt Stack

thirty-minute swim in the super-chilly San Francisco Bay and
an hour-and-a-half bike ride. During much of the year, all of
this is followed by a full day's work as a hod carrier. Saturdays
and Sundays are saved for a race.

Now 72 years old, Walt began running at age 58. He sums up
the effects of his first weeks of jogging as a bout with Irish
arthritis: "stiffness in every joint but one." Ever the organizer,

Walt founded and remains as president of the San Francisco Dolphin South End club, one of the more colorful and widely known of all running clubs.

Ed Asner

Actor Ed Asner may never be a long-distance runner, but taking up jogging a couple of miles a day five years ago may have greatly prolonged his life. At the time, the star of the televison series "Lou Grant" was forty pounds overweight, and his doctor had discovered a rare abnormality in his heart beat called a right bundle-branch block.

He knew he had to shape up, but he was embarrassed. "I was carrying a lot of extra weight and I was afraid people would make fun of me if I ran on the streets. So I began running in my back yard, about twenty laps a day, which equaled a mile."

As the excess fat began melting away, a more confident Asner went public and began pounding the streets around his Hollywood Hills home.

Some months and many pounds later, his heart specialist again put Asner through a grueling twenty-minute treadmill test. To the doctor's amazement his heart aberration had vanished—the only explanation was that running was easing the heart problem.

The 49-year-old Asner summed up his feelings regarding his early morning ritual, "The clearest statement I can make about running is that no matter how tired it might make me the rest of the day (I am always happy to sit down whenever I can while working) my appreciation of being alive is much more intense."

Jim Hershberger

Wichita oilman Jim Hershberger has been a prime mover in the growth of running in the Midwest, an extremely benevolent man who has donated much time and money. He is competitive at distances from 100 yards to the marathon, setting Missouri Valley A.A.U. records in fourteen different distances at age 43 alone to become Distance Athlete of the Year in 1975.

But running, which had been such an important part of his life off and on (owing to frequent injuries and business involvements) since 1947, became, during a recent tragic period, a vital center which Jim Hershberger credits with helping him see his way through surgery, the deaths of his parents, the death of his oldest son, and serious accidents involving two other sons. Throughout, the eighty miles he put in each week helped him avoid succumbing to despair.

Allan Angoff

Crowded conditions at his usual exercise haunt, the swimming pool at the Upper Montclair, New Jersey, YMCA, forced Allan Angoff out onto the track. The freedom of the road suited him and he has been running three to five miles six days a week for the past three years.

The 60-year-old administrator of the American Parapsychology Foundation and author of several books including *Psychic Force* feels that, "What I achieve in running is not really related to physical fitness. Running may not add a moment to my life. But it doesn't matter, in running I become at one with the universe, I become detached from the office routine, from the workaday cares. I enter into a sublime environment in which I discover my identity. It is beyond physical fitness and health and doctors and long life and beating the calendar. Rather, it is the blithe spirit, and I soar even if I do not fly, I achieve what Thoreau called 'absolute freedom and wildness.' "

Ruth Anderson

One of the highlights Ruth Anderson remembers best is a 100-K run around San Francisco's Lake Merced in 1976. She began running in predawn dark on a foggy December morning and finished in postdusk dark. The twenty-six laps around the five-mile circuit passed with surprisingly little discomfort; she even freshened quite a bit at the 50-K mark.

Since then, Ruth Anderson has completed several more ultramarathons, more than thirty marathons, and numerous races of shorter length in the United States and abroad. Not bad for a

Ruth Anderson

radiochemist who began running only after coworkers at Lawrence Livermore Laboratories talked her into joining their lunchtime runs three years earlier. She is now welcomed everywhere as a most gracious ambassador of women's master running, one who has been successful both in attracting more women to the sport and in increasing the consideration shown women competitors at meets.

Fritz Mueller

The success of masters runner Fritz Mueller takes the punch out of that most commonly used excuse not to try competitive running—"I started out too late in life."

Mueller, who is 46, did not begin running until the summer of 1973. He says, "As a runner I am young. . . I have the advantage of still being driven to get better as a young runner does."

Better and better he became—in 1978 he ran to United States Masters championships in the marathon and the 50-kilometer divisions. He turned in a blistering 2:20:47 at Boston, establishing an American masters record.

Mueller has tenaciously tackled the open division feeling that "runners should find anyone in the race fair game regardless of age." His true grit earned him first place against all comers in the 1978 running of the grueling Yonkers Marathon.

In 1979 Mueller finished Boston on the heels of a new masters runner, Herb Lorenz (who had turned 40 earlier that month). He accepted second place philosophically and views it as a motivating factor for his continued running progress. He does not plan to change his training radically; he still trains according to how he feels.

Mueller has apparently continued to feel fine. . . in his six short years of pounding out the miles, he has become one of the most respected racers in both U.S. and international competition.

George P. Reeder

On doctor's orders to lose weight and lower his blood pressure, at age 64 retired aircraft executive George Reeder began running. Two and one-half years later his perseverance has paid off—he is thirty pounds lighter and much more relaxed.

Reeder follows a self-designed morning regimen that consists of calisthenics (including forty sit-ups) a three- to five-mile run, and then a ten-mile exercycle ride back at home.

He runs by himself, "Running alone gives a person my age the prerogative of setting the pace most comfortable for me." He adds that the consistency of his work-outs and finding the right pair of shoes have been key factors in his continued progress.

For Reeder that progress came slowly—having to start at the beginning after a fifty-year layoff (the last time he actively pursued the sport was as a teenager in high school). He found that he didn't need any gimmicks to keep him out there trying, "Running magazines and books add a little spice, but if after six months you still need motivation—see your undertaker."

The routine he began begrudgingly, he now looks forward to, "I feel that the self-confidence and greatly improved health will keep me running for many years to come. I have learned how to push myself—each day I can feel my wind improve."

For the beginning over-forty runner Reeder offers this simple advice: "Be tenacious." The reasons people take up running are as varied as the people themselves. Reeder put it this way, "I run now only for good health and well being—after thirty-one years behind a desk, I have learned to value the rewards of activity. I run to please myself, and I find that in the world of sports this is one in which I can be my own hero—because of my improved fitness and self-confidence."

David H. Wilson

David Wilson, a forty-one-year-old performance analyst for a major airline, has only been running for three years. In that short time, however, he has participated in many 10-kilometer races and marathons—including Boston—and has a respectable best marathon time of 3:22.

A desire to improve physical fitness prompted Wilson to begin running in 1976. As his daily mileage increased from one-half mile to approximately ten miles (he now puts in six to nine miles each weekday and fifteen on Saturday and Sunday), he discovered that he *did* feel better physically as well as psychologically. He kicked a two pack-a-day cigarette habit, cut down his liquor consumption, improved his eating habits, and became calmer and more relaxed in his everyday life.

Encouraged by his friends and tolerated by his family, Wilson has found that running has become an important facet of his

David Wilson

life. He does say, however: "I recommend that running be kept in the proper perspective with the runner's overall lifestyle. Otherwise, the pure joy and well-being derived from running becomes lost."

The fact that he runs at 4:30 a.m. explains why he usually runs alone. He stresses the importance of stretching before and after running, the purchase of *good* running shoes, and his standard advice on injury prevention, "Don't do too much too fast." Although he has not suffered any major injuries, he has learned his body stress levels and is careful not to exceed his limits.

Wilson also adds, "I would like to see more AAU financial support and backing of Master's Olympics and annual world-wide competition."

He lives in Manhattan Beach, California, where he is a member of the Seniors Track Club.

Erich Segal

A canoe accident in 1953 caused sixteen-year-old Erich Segal to seek physical therapy to rebuild his injured leg. He started running and never stopped, including twenty straight Boston Marathons. He has accumulated numerous trophies and has turned in many outstanding performances running, but his fame comes from his literary works, most notably *Love Story*.

His advice to masters runners: "Stretch more than you ever did. Warm down after a run. Don't be suckered into wearing light shoes; you need all the protection you can get for your aging legs."

Herb Lorenz

For the first fifteen or so years of his running career, Herb Lorenz was a man without a distance—he had tried them all. While he did well when he ran, he still had not found the one event at which he could excel—until 1970. That was the year Lorenz ran his first marathon.

The race he chose, the hilly Yonkers marathon, was no easy course. He won in 2:28 and "felt great about it. I was strong at the end and felt that this was my distance."

The path to Lorenz' initial marathon victory began at Trenton State College. There, with no previous running background, he went out for track and proved to be a natural. His training technique consisted solely of running fast intervals. He ran the half-mile and mile with best collegiate times of 1:53 and 4:13.

Lorenz' post graduation position as vocational arts instructor at a New Jersey high school was ideal. He found plenty of students eager to pace him on the school track.

Next, he was persuaded to try the steeplechase. He ran three with the last at the Olympic Trials in 1964. Lorenz placed 8th but developed problems with his Achilles tendon. "I couldn't even walk. It became an on-and-off type thing."

Following his foray into steeplechasing Lorenz began another adventure which proved to be easier on his injured legs and longer lasting. He started road racing. Over the next half dozen years he was a consistent winner in road races in the Middle Atlantic AAU region. His best road distances seemed to be 15- and 20-kilometers.

In addition to road racing, Lorenz got hooked on cross-country, with equal success. He once placed as high as sixteenth in the National AAU Cross-Country Championships.

Lorenz credits his ultimate success with the marathon distance to his turning away from the interval training that dominated his early years. Boston 1979 was Lorenz' first marathon in the masters category—he was 40 years and 9 days old. Winning with a time of 2:24:41 wasn't up to his high expectations though—"I was hoping to do it faster. I thought maybe I could go under 2:20 that day."

The 2:20 goal was no idle runners's daydream. Since his first race at Yonkers, Lorenz has run more than twenty marathons. He holds the U.S. record for age 36 (a 2:17:43 at Boston) and for age 32 (oddly, a slower 2:19:17).

Steering his two young children away from running is no easy task, but Lorenz does. He feels that his lack of running as a youngster has contributed greatly to his longevity and success in the sport. "The kids have grown up with running. It was here before they were, and it will always be in our family."

Paul Reese

In 1963, Paul Reese's 16-year-old son took up running, and Paul, facing retirement from the Marine Corps, decided to take it up too. One hundred and eleven marathons later, Paul and son Mark finished the same 50-mile run; Mark in 6:50, Paul in 7:32. At one time they held the father-and-son marathon record.

An active member of the Buffalo Chips running club of

Paul Reese

Sacramento, California, Paul is a marathon reader as well as a marathon runner. He keeps up with virtually everything published on running and writes a column for the local newspaper. Also, he prefers running with family members or friends to running alone so that he can discuss running.

What does such a storehouse of running knowledge suggest are the means for preventing injury? "Youth and stretching exercises, both of which elude me."

Ken Mueller

Ken Mueller

Forty-one-year-old Ken Mueller has been running since junior high track, leading, in recent years, to several championships, age-group records, and the American record for a forty year old in the marathon: 2:27:55 (surpassed by Herb Lorenz in 1979). He posted a 2:22:26 in the 1975 Boston Marathon but missed the 1976 Olympic trials because of an injury. He owes these accomplishments to the eighty-plus miles he puts in each week through the woods near his Bellingham, Massachusetts, home, often accompanied by his wife or daughters.

Monday, Wednesday, and Friday see him take easy ten-mile runs. Tuesday, Thursday, and Saturday he tackles a hard ten- or twelve-mile run with hill pickups. Sundays find him putting in eighteen miles or better. Plus, he gets in about three cross-country races each month.

Alan Cranston

Whoever says that politicians lounge around all day on cushioned chairs behind ponderous walnut desks and then move on only to lean on heavily varnished mahogany bars all night has obviously never met Alan Cranston.

The senior senator from California defies most political stereotypes. Cranston is a runner and has been for the majority of his 65 years. From his boyhood days at Los Altos, California, elementary school to his early glory years at Mountain View High, to his current daily runs in Washington, D.C. and occasional races, running has become an established and permanent part of his life.

The tall, lean Democrat begins his one-hour runs at 6:30 a.m. He finds that his notoriety has become a problem, he frequently encounters gawkers, admirers, and autograph seekers. "It's difficult not to stop when someone recognizes you," said Cranston. "You don't want to offend a constituent."

Usually, says Cranston, he is concentrating so hard on his running that he doesn't notice people noticing him.

He knows how to push himself—much the way he did in 1932. At that time he was Santa Clara County high school champion in the 100 yard dash (10.1 seconds) and 440 (54.0).

A standout on the Stanford University track teams of the mid-1930s, he participated in the 1936 U.S. Olympic Games trials nearly winning himself a trip to Berlin.

Recently he encountered a new problem. His press secretary wanted him to regain some of the 21 pounds he has shed since increasing his mileage so that he would look better on tele-vision. Cranston refused fearing it would slow him down and "besides it's downright unhealthy." His doctor confirmed that he is in excellent health with a low pulse and significantly lower than normal blood pressure for his age.

His tough senate record proves that there is a politician under that relaxed non-aggressive personality. But it surfaces only when Cranston isn't wearing his track suit.

Galen Blackmore

Galen Blackmore, who has been running the last fifty-three of his sixty-three years despite a brief layoff in 1959 for successful surgery and radiation treatment for a serious form of cancer, knows what it takes for the older runner to stay motivated. "Always keep in mind the values of running. I feel that a person who continues to run after forty or who takes up running after forty has found the so-called fountain of youth."

In Blackmore's case, that youthfulness is fully evidenced by a physique and vigor of a much younger person, as well as a keen awareness of fitness. He is retiring this year from a forty-year career as a junior high school physical education instructor, athletic director, and coach of various sports including track at the junior and senior high school levels in El Dorado, Kansas. Over the years he has been actively involved in such things as the development of the local high school cross-country running program, and the city's widely popular summer recreation program.

His running history has included setting the Kansas state high school record for the half mile in 1934 (1:58.2), a record that was unbeaten on the state level for eleven years, was the fastest half-mile time that year in the nation, and was a local school record not broken until 1979. He lettered all four years in track at Kansas State University of Pittsburg, where his two-mile relay team won numerous races at the Kansas Relays, Drake Relays, Illinois Relays, and other meets.

Today he follows a relatively light workout schedule emphasizing stretching that he complements with calisthenics, weight training, and hiking with his beagles. He doesn't currently compete, but says he would like to enter Masters races after retirement, preferring the short to mid distances rather than marathons. Basically, he runs for health benefits, endurance and strength, and because "I have always enjoyed running."

Bill Gookin

Bill Gookin

Bill Gookin is most widely known as the marketing force behind Gookinaid, an electrolyte-replacement drink popular with runners. But that is just an interesting sidelight to a running career that dates back to high-school track in 1950, including major achievements at every step and two presidencies of the San Diego Track Club.

The nature of his commitments forces many layoffs, which doesn't seem to bother Bill too much; he actually looks forward to coming back after a layoff: "I feel so much better. The newly sore muscles give me a good feeling. My mental outlook becomes more relaxed, and I feel less lethargic."

John F. Smith

Jack Smith's doctor advised him that "a man of your age [42 at the time] should get some exercise. Singles tennis would be too strenuous, but doubles might be okay." He was still smarting from that advice when he bought a copy of *Aerobics* and quickly became hooked on running. Now, after thirteen years of running, Smith is enjoying better health than ever before.

He credits running for his ability to work longer and harder, the disappearance of his allergies, and an appearance years younger than that of his contemporaries who do not run. When not running or serving as a senior research chemical engineer, he takes off on canoeing and camping trips.

Jack Smith keeps track of his running by time, not distance. Fifteen to twenty-five minutes of running each weekday is topped off with a forty-five minute run on Saturdays. Sunday is a day of rest unless there is a fun run scheduled nearby.

In spite of his dedication to the sport, Smith refuses to run in ice, snow, or cold rain, so his schedule in winter is often interrupted by inclement weather. When he does run, however, he runs alone and prefers training between 5:30 and 6:30 a.m. because of the "solitude and clean air." Smith keeps a personal training diary which he feels keeps him motivated—his before and after weight and measurements have convinced and encouraged him to keep moving.

"Set both short- and long-term goals for yourself," advises Smith, "then work toward both. Learn to relax and enjoy running for it's own sake. The other benefits that accrue are fringe benefits."

Smith belongs to the Amazing Feet Running Club in New Providence, New Jersey, and has run several 10,000 meter races. He finished third in the Master's class in his most recent attempt. He states, "There should be more Master's-only races and they should be divided by five-year spans whenever possible. There is a big difference between 51 and 59 years, for example."

Appendix

Masters Records

MEN'S MASTERS RECORDS
COMPILED BY PETER MUNDLE

These pages contain the known world age records in every standard men's track and field event, age 35 and above, as of December 31, 1978. If an American does not hold the world record, his mark is listed after the world record holder's.

Information, from left to right: age, performance, athlete's name and residence.

Key to abbreviations: N = Non-winning time; H = Heat; M = Metric event; I = Indoor mark; Dec. = Mark made in decathlon; Pen. = Mark made in Pentathlon; W = Wind-assisted mark; Exh. = Mark made in exhibition race; Y = Mark recorded during an English measurement (yards, feet, miles) race, or in the case of the One-Hour Run, all distances are given in English measurements; P = Verification of birthdate, etc. pending.

Published in 1979 by Tafnews Press, Book Division of Track & Field News, P.O. Box 296, Los Altos, California 94022 USA.

MASTERS AGE RECORDS 1979 is an official publication of the National Amateur Athletic Union (AAU) Masters Track & Field Committee, Robert Fine, Chairman, National sponsor of the Masters Track & Field Committee is Occidental Life of North Carolina.

100 YARDS

Age	Mark	Athlete
35	9.6	Clifton Bertrand (Trinidad; New York)
	10.1	Kenneth Dennis (California)
	10.1	Bob Warren (Iowa)
	10.1	Maurice McDonald (North Carolina)
36	9.6	Clifton Bertrand (Trinidad; New York)
	10.1	Kenneth Dennis (California)
37	9.7	Walt Butler (California)
38	9.9 N	Percy Knox (California)
39	9.9	Dean Smith (California)
	9.9	Robert Thomas (New York)
40	9.9	Robert Thomas (New York)
	9.9	Percy Knox (California)
	9.9	Jim Weaver (Texas)

Age	Mark	Name
41	9.8 WN	Percy Knox (California)
	9.6 Exh.	Charles Beaudry (Texas)
42	9.8	Percy Knox (California)
43	9.8	Thane Baker (Texas)
	10.1	Percy Knox (California)
44	10.0	Percy Knox (California)
45	10.3 H	Richard Stolpe (Nebraska)
	10.3	Thane Baker (Texas)
46	10.0	Thane Baker (Texas)
47	10.7	Milford Parker (New York)
48	10.5 N	Jack Greenwood (Kansas)
	10.5	Edmund Schuler (Florida)
49	10.5	Edmund Schuler (Florida)
50	10.5	Alphonse Juilland (California)
51	10.5	Edmund Schuler (Florida)
52	10.6	Rudolph Valentine (New York)
53	10.9	Rudolph Valentine (New York)
	10.8 WN	Robert McDonald (California)
54	10.8	Alfred Guidet (California)
55	10.7	Payton Jordan (California)
	10.7	Alfred Guidet (California)
	10.7	Charles Beaudry (Texas)
56	10.7	Payton Jordan (California)
	10.5 W	Alfred Guidet (California)
57	10.7	Payton Jordan (California)
58	10.8	Payton Jordan (California)
59	10.8	Payton Jordan (California)
60	11.1	Payton Jordan (California)
61	10.9	Payton Jordan (California)
62	12.2	Virgil McIntyre (Arizona)
	12.2	George Braceland (Pennsylvania)
	12.2	W. J. Seldon (Texas)
	11.8 W	Fritiof Sjostrand (Sweden;California)
63	12.4	A. J. Puglizevich
64	11.8	Harry Koppel (California)
65	12.3	Ken Carnine (California)
	12.3	Fred White (Texas)
	12.1 W	Ken Carnine (California)

Age	Mark	Name
66	12.3	Ken Carnine (California)
67	12.5 N	Ken Carnine (California)
68	12.5	Ken Carnine (California)
69	12.5	Ken Carnine (California)
70	13.6	Sing Lum (California)
	13.1 W	Sing Lum (California)
71	13.7	Sing Lum (California)
	13.5 W	Sing Lum (California)
72	13.6	Konrad Boas (United States)
73	13.7	Sing Lum (California)
	13.7	Sing Lum (California)
74	13.7	Josiah Packard (California)
75	13.4	Herbert Anderson (Colorado)
76	22.5	Paul Spangler (California)
	P18.5	Guy Paschall (United States)
	19.5 W	Paul Spangler (California)
77	15.6	Buell Crane (Idaho)
78	15.4	Buell Crane (Idaho)
79	16.6	Ted Mumby (California)
	P13.2 N	Duncan McClean (Great Britain)
88	17.1	Duncan McClean (Great Britain)

100 METERS

Age	Mark	Name
35	10.3 N	Arquimedes Herrera (Venezuela)
	10.3	Edward Jefferis (South Africa)
	10.4 NI	Mel Pender (United States Army)
36	10.4	Rafael Fortun (Cuba)
	11.1	Bob Warren (Iowa)
37	10.5	Walt Butler (California)
38	10.6 H	Edward Jefferis (South Africa)
	10.8	Kenneth Dennis (California)
39	10.5 H	David James (United States; Switzerland)
40	10.8	Reginald Austin (Australia)
	10.9	Jim Weaver (Texas)
	10.7 W	Robert Whilden (Texas)

Age	Time	Name
41	10.7	Thane Baker (Texas)
42	11.1	Edmund Burg (West Germany)
	11.1	Thane Baker (Texas)
	11.1	Vandolph Parish (California)
	11.0 W	Robert Thomas (New York)
43	11.0	Percy Knox (California)
	10.9 W	Thane Baker (Texas)
44	11.0	Percy Knox (California)
45	11.1 N	George Rhoden (Jamaica; California)
	11.4 N	Richard Stolpe (Nebraska)
	11.4	Dick Marlin (California)
46	11.4	Robert Messersmith (California)
	11.2	Charles Williams (Great Britain)
	11.3	Thane Baker (Texas)
47	11.3 N	Richard Stolpe (Nebraska)
48	11.4	Richard Stolpe (Nebraska)
49	P11.3 H	Rocky McPherson (Guyana)
	11.3	Peter Mirkes (West Germany)
	11.5 N	Alphonse Juilland (California)
	11.3 WH	Jack Greenwood (Kansas)
50	11.4 N	Alphonse Juilland (California)
51	11.5	Richard Stolpe (New Mexico)
52	11.5	Richard Stolpe (New Mexico)
53	12.2 H	Alfred Guidet (California)
	12.2	Richard Stolpe (New Mexico)
54	11.7	Payton Jordan (California)
55	11.6	Payton Jordan (California)
56	11.6 N	Payton Jordan (California)
	11.5 W	Alfred Guidet (California)
57	11.6	Bernard Hogan (Australia)
58	11.9	Payton Jordan (California)
59	11.7	Payton Jordan (California)
60	12.0	Payton Jordan (California)
61	11.8	Payton Jordan (California)
62	12.3 H	Fritz Assmy (West Germany)
	12.8	Virgil McIntyre (Arizona)
63	12.6	Yngve Brange (Sweden)
	13.3	Fred White (Texas)
64	12.9	Yngve Brange (Sweden)
	12.9	Harry Koppel (California)
65	12.8	Yngve Brange (Sweden)
	13.0	Harry Koppel (California)
66	13.4 N	Joe Caruso (California)
67	13.5	Alois Brhluk (Czechoslovakia)
	13.7	Anthony Castro (California)
	13.5 W	Ken Carnine (California)
	13.5N	Ken Carnine (California)
68	13.5	Anthony Castro (California)
	13.4	Frederick Reid (California)
69	14.6	George Simpson (Australia)
70	14.6	Sing Lum (California)
	14.6	Manfred D'Elia (New Jersey)
	14.4 W	Winfield McFadden (California)
71	14.5 N	Sing Lum (California)
	14.5	Winfield McFadden (California)
72	15.0	Sing Lum (California)
	15.0	Winfield McFadden (California)
	P14.3 W	Josiah Packard (Hawaii)
73	13.9	Josiah Packard (California)
74	14.2 Dec.	Herbert Anderson (Colorado)
75	14.6	Herbert Anderson (Colorado)
76	15.4	Herbert Anderson (Colorado)
77	16.5	Buell Crane (Idaho)
	P15.6 N	H. Okada (Japan)
	P15.1 W	H. Okada (Japan)
78	17.5 N	Ted Mumby (California)
79	19.4	Ted Mumby (California)
82	20.5	Charles Backus (United States)
83	20.2	Collister Wheeler (Oregon)
84	19.9 N	Charley Speechly (Great Britain)
	23.4	Charles Backus (United States)
87	19.3 N	Duncan McClean (Great Britain)
88	16.3 N	Duncan McClean (Great Britain)

No.	Time	Name
89	16.5	Duncan McClean (Great Britain)
90	19.9	Duncan McClean (Great Britain)
91	21.0	Duncan McClean (Great Britain)
92	21.7	Duncan McClean (Great Britain)
93	P21.7	Duncan McClean (Great Britain)

200 METERS - 220 YARDS

No.	Time	Name
35	21.7 M	Edward Jefferis (South Africa)
	P21.3 M	Hendrickson Harewood (Trinidad)
	22.4 M	Ron Whitney (California)
36	21.6	Clifton Bertrand (Trinidad; New York)
	22.2	Arnold Budd (New York)
37	21.6 M	Edward Jefferis (South Africa)
	21.9 MN	Kenneth Dennis (California)
38	21.3 M	Ed Jeffreys (South Africa)
	20.6 W	Reginald Austin (Australia)
	22.1 M	Kenneth Dennis (California)
39	21.3 M	Edward Jefferis (South Africa)
	21.9 M	Kenneth Dennis (California)
	22.0	Robert Thomas (New York)
40	21.9 M	Reginald Austin (Australia)
	22.3 M	Dean Smith (California)
	22.4	Jim Weaver (Texas)
41	22.2 M	Ron Taylor (Great Britain)
	22.4 M	Dean Smith (California)
42	22.3	Thane Baker (Texas)
43	22.7 M	Ron Taylor (Great Britain)
	22.9 M	James Lingel (California)
	22.5 WNM	Thane Baker (Texas)
44	22.9 MH	George Rhoden (Jamaica; California)
	22.9 M	Milton Newton (California)
	22.8 WMH	Hans Bruhner (Sweden; California)`
45	22.3 MN	George Rhoden (Jamaica; California)
	22.9 M	Richard Stolpe (Nebraska)
46	22.9 M	Charles Williams (Great Britain)

No.	Time	Name
47	23.1	Thane Baker (Texas)
	23.4 M	Charles Williams (Great Britain)
	23.4 MN	Richard Stolpe (Nebraska)
48	P23.1 MH	Rocky McPherson (Guyana)
	23.2 M	Richard Stolpe (Nebraska)
49	23.6 MN	Alphonse Juilland (California)
	23.2 WM	Jack Greenwood (Kansas)
50	23.6 M	Jack Greenwood (Kansas)
51	23.7 M	Jack Greenwood (Kansas)
52	23.9 M	Richard Stolpe (New Mexico)
53	24.6	Rudolph Valentine (New York)
54	23.6 M	Payton Jordan (California)
55	23.6 M	Alfred Guiden (California)
56	24.2	Charles Beaudry (Texas)
	24.2	Payton Jordan (California)
57	24.3 N	Alfred Guidet (California)
58	25.9 M	Alfred Guidet (California)
59	25.5	Fritiof Sjostrand (Sweden; California)
	27.0	Virgil McIntyre (Arizona)
60	24.9 M	Payton Jordan (California)
61	25.0 M	Payton Jordan (California)
62	26.0 M	Fritz Assmy (West Germany)
	25.9 WM	Fritiof Sjostrand (Sweden; California)
	27.0 M	Virgil McIntyre (Arizona)
63	26.7 M	Fritz Assmy (West Germany)
	27.4 M	Fred White (Texas)
64	27.1	Fritiof Sjostrand (Sweden; California)
65	28.4	Ken Carnine (California)
	27.6 M	Yngve Brange (Sweden)
	27.7 M	Harry Koppel (California)
	27.4 WM	Harry Koppel (California)
66	28.3 M	Virgil McIntyre (Arizona)
67	28.6 M	Richard Lacey (New York)
	28.3 WMN	Ken Carnine (California)
68	28.1 MN	Ken Carnine (California)
69	28.5 M	Frederick Reid (California)
70	30.1 M	Manfred D'Elia (New Jersey)
71	30.4 M	Winfield McFadden (California)

Age	Time	Name
72	31.4 M	Winfield McFadden (California)
73	29.2 M	Josiah Packard (California)
	29.0 WM	Josiah Packard (California)
74	30.2 M	Josiah Packard (California)
75	31.0	Herbert Anderson (Colorado)
76	33.4 M	Herbert Anderson (Colorado)
77	35.2 M	Alfred Sutherland (Great Britain)
	35.6 M	Buell Crane (Idaho)
78	39.1 M	Buell Crane (Idaho)
79	41.9	Ted Mumby (California)
80	41.2 M	Sven Falk (Sweden)
83	42.1 M	Collister Wheeler (Oregon)
84	43.1 MN	Charley Speechly (Great Britain)
	58.7 WM	Charles Backus (United States)
87	41.1 MN	Duncan McClean (Great Britain)
88	45.9 MN	Duncan McClean (Great Britain)
89	44.8 MN	Duncan McClean (Great Britain)
90	49.2 M	Duncan McClean (Great Britain)
91	51.5	Duncan McClean (Great Britain)

Age	Time	Name
42	50.5 M	Gerald Leroy (Great Britain)
	51.4 M	Robert Thomas (New York)
43	52.1 M	Keith Whitaker (Great Britain)
	52.5 M	Milton Newton (California)
44	51.6 M	Milton Newton (California)
45	52.1 M	Johan Hesselberg (Norway)
	52.4 M	Don Cheek (California)
46	52.2 M	Bill Fitzgerald (California)
47	51.7 M	Richard Stolpe (Nebraska)
48	52.4 MN	Richard Stolpe (Nebraska)
49	52.0 M	Jack Greenwood (Kansas)
50	53.6 M	Jack Greenwood (Kansas)
51	52.9 M	Jack Greenwood (Kansas)
52	53.9 M	Jack Greenwood (Kansas)
53	54.6	Rudolph Valentine (New York)
54	54.5 M	Rudolph Valentine (New York)
55	54.8 M	Rudolph Valentine (New York)
56	56.5	Charles Beaudry (Texas)
57	56.4	Alfred Guidet (California)
58	58.3	Ray Gordon (Washington DC)
59	58.8 M	Fritiof Sjostrand (Sweden; California)
	62.8 Dec.	Virgil McIntyre (Arizona)
60	59.1 M	Russel Niblock (Washington)
61	59.8 M	Fritiof Sjostrand (Sweden; California)
	62.5	Bud Deacon (Hawaii)
62	59.7 M	Fritiof Sjostrand (Sweden; California)
	62.4 Dec.	Bud Deacon (Hawaii)
63	62.0 M	Fritz Assmy (West Germany)
	62.3 Dec.	Bud Deacon (Hawaii)
64	61.5	Fritiof Sjostrand (Sweden; California)
	65.5 Dec.	Bud Deacon (Hawaii)
65	64.0 M	Harry Koppel (California)
66	65.8 MN	Merv Jenkinson (Australia)
	66.9 M	Mel Shine (California)
67	66.7	Richard Lacey (New York)
68	65.5 M	Ken Carnine (California)
69	70.0 M	Fritz Philipps (West Germany)
	70.4 M	Sydney Madden (California)

400 METERS - 440 YARDS

Age	Time	Name
35	47.0	Hagues Roger (France)
	48.9 M	Ron Whitney (California)
36	48.2 M	Johannes Cyrus (South Africa)
	51.3	Maurice McDonald (United States)
37	48.6 M	Ron Taylor (Great Britain)
	51.1 M	Maurice McDonald (North Carolina)
38	50.9 M	Gary Miller (Jamaica)
39	49.9 M	Mal Spence (Jamaica)
	51.5	Cliff Cordy (California)
40	49.5 M	Noel Clough (Australia)
	50.8 M	Gary Miller (California)
41	49.7 M	Jim Dixon (Great Britain)
	51.0 M	Ray Adams (Washington DC)
	51.0 M	John Sanders (Pennsylvania)

Age	Time	Name
70	68.4 MN	Harold Chapson (Hawaii)
71	67.2 M	Harold Chapson (Hawaii)
72	68.1 M	Harold Chapson (Hawaii)
73	64.6 M	Josiah Packard (California)
74	68.9 M	Harold Chapson (Hawaii)
75	69.9 M	Herbert Anderson (Colorado)
76	76.8 M	Herbert Anderson (Colorado)
77	92.0 M	Paul Spangler (California)
79	91.1 M	Paul Spangler (California)
82	2:16.7 M	Charles Backus (United States)
83	2:20.9 M	Charles Backus (United States)
84	.2:29.2 M	Charles Backus (United States)

800 METERS - 880 YARDS

Age	Time	Name
35	1:49.2	George Scott (California)
	1:55.0 M	Ron Whitney (California)
36	1:53.2 M	Mario Lanzi (Italy)
	P1:52.8 M	Anthony Elgie (Great Britain)
	1:58.6 MN	Larry Bridges (New Mexico)
37	1:52.5 M	Hubert Streit (West Germany)
	1:58.0 M	Cliff Cordy (California)
38	1:52.8 M	Michel Bernard (France)
	2:00.6 MN	Arthur Conro (Massachusetts)
39	1:56.6 M	Noel Clough (Australia)
	1:58.5 M	Cliff Cordy (California)
40	1:54.8 M	Noel Clough (Australia)
	1:58.8 NH	Frank McBride (Michigan)
41	1:54.5 M	Klaus Mainka (West Germany)
	1:57.5 M	Ernest Billups (Illinois)
42	1:58.2 M	David Pratt (California)
43	1:57.9 M	Tom Roberts (Australia)
	2:02.2 N	Willis Kleinsasser (California)
44	1:59.8	Bill Fitzgerald (California)
	1:57.9 H	Rune Hesselberg (Norway)
45	2:01.4 N	Bill Fitzgerald (California)
46	1:59.9 M	Ed Whitlock (Canada)
	2:00.9	Bill Fitzgerald (California)
47	1:58.4 M	Bill Fitzgerald (California)
48	1:58.1 MN	Bill Fitzgerald (California)
49	1:59.5 MN	Bill Fitzgerald (California)
50	2:01.1 M	Bill Fitzgerald (California)
51	2:03.2 M	Bill Fitzgerald (California)
52	2:04.0 M	Dean Smith (Illinois)
53	2:07.1 MN	Wally Sheppard (Australia)
	2:09.0 M	George Puterbaugh (Oregon)
54	2:13.5 MH	Archie Messenger (New York)
55	2:11.9 M	John Gilmour (Australia)
	2:13.5 N	Ray Gordon (Washington DC)
56	2:12.9 M	John Gilmour (Australia)
	2:16.2 M	Richmond Morcom (Pennsylvania)
57	2:17.2 M	Henry Fairbank (North Carolina)
58	2:14.5 M	John Gilmour (Australia)
	2:18.0 MH	Henry Fairbank (North Carolina)
59	2:18.0 M	John Gilmour (Australia)
60	2:20.5 N	Ray Gordon (Virginia)
61	2:19.9 N	Ray Gordon (Virginia)
	2:19.9 M	George Buck (Australia)
	2:23.8	Bud Deacon (Hawaii)
62	2:22.8 M	George Buck (Australia)
	2:26.6	Bud Deacon (Hawaii)
63	2:23.1	Bud Deacon (Hawaii)
64	2:27.2 M	William Andberg (Minnesota)
65	2:27.2 M	Norman Bright (Washington)
66	2:28.0 M	William Andberg (Minnesota)
67	2:30.2 M	William Andberg (Minnesota)
68	2:32.8 M	Merv Jenkinson (Australia)
	2:36.0 H	Sydney Madden (California)
69	2:38.7 MN	Richard Bredenbeck (Ohio)
70	2:37.0 M	Harold Chapson (Hawaii)
71	2:34.5 M	Monty Montgomery (California)
72	2:35.4 M	Harold Chapson (Hawaii)
73	2:35.8 M	Harold Chapson (Hawaii)
74	2:37.2 M	Harold Chapson (Hawaii)

Age	Time	Name
75	2:40.0 M	Harold Chapson (Hawaii)
76	3:17.9 M	Lou Gregory (Florida)
77	3:20.3 MN	Paul Spangler (California)
78	3:17.9 M	Paul Spangler (California)
79	3:18.0 M	Paul Spangler (California)
83	5:53.0 M	Charles Backus (United States)
90	8:54.2 M	Robert Willis (California)

1500 METERS

Age	Time	Name
35	3:46.0	Gerard Vervoort (France)
36	4:06.3	Tom Richards (California)
	3:46.1	Gerard Vervoort (France)
	4:03.6	Larry Bridges (New Mexico)
37	3:42.4	Gerard Vervoort (France)
	4:07.2	William Hall (North Carolina)
	P4:05.1	Ralph Lee (United States)
38	3:45.5	Gerard Vervoort (France)
	4:08.5	Jack Knebel (California)
39	3:52.7	Michel Bernard (France)
	4:07.0 N	Bill Gookin (California)
40	3:52.0	Michel Bernard (France)
	4:05.9	Wilbur Williams (California)
41	3:56.7	Clement Huyssen (Belgium)
	4:06.9 N	Glynn Wood (Washington DC)
42	3:58.8	Albie Thomas (Australia)
	4:10.5	James Vantatenhove (California)
43	3:59.5	Jim McDonald (New Zealand)
	4:07.4	Glynn Wood (Washington DC)
44	4:01.2	Laurie O'Hara (Great Britain)
	4:06.1 N	Hal Higdon (Indiana)
45	4:03.2	Piet Mayoor (Holland)
	4:13.6	Bill Fitzgerald (California)
46	4:06.1	Ed Whitlock (Canada)
	4:18.1	Ken Napier (Nevada)
47	4:10.4 N	Bill Fitzgerald (California)
48	4:12.1 N	Bill Fitzgerald (California)
49	4:12.9 N	Bill Fitzgerald (California)
50	4:15.0	Theo Orr (Australia)
	4:18.6	Bill Fitzgerald (California)
51	4:18.5	Bill Fitzgerald (California)
52	4:14.6 N	Jack Ryan (Australia)
	4:29.3	Dean Smith (Illinois)
53	4:14.0	Jack Ryan (Australia)
	4:30.2 N	Mauro Hernandes (California)
	4:25.0 N	George McGrath (Australia)
54	4:36.3	Mauro Hernandes (California)
55	4:20.7	Jack Ryan (Australia)
	4:29.7	Mauro Hernandes (California)
56	4:22.0	John Gilmour (Australia)
	4:34.5	Mauro Hernandes (California)
57	4:24.0	John Gilmour (Australia)
	4:41.9 N	George Sheehan (New Jersey)
58	4:28.3	John Gilmour (Australia)
	4:54.2 N	Ray Mahannah (California)
59	4:27.0	John Gilmour (Australia)
	4:53.0 N	Ray Gordon (Virginia)
60	4:50.3	Ole Elvland (Sweden)
	4:58.0	Clive Davies (Oregon)
61	4:51.3	Jan Verloop (Netherlands)
	4:53.2	William Andberg (Minnesota)
62	4:49.8	Don Longenecker (New Mexico)
63	4:53.5	William Andberg (Minnesota)
64	5:01.3	William Andberg (Minnesota)
65	4:59.2	William Andberg (Minnesota)
66	5:03.3	William Andberg (Minnestoa)
	5:04.8	Merv Jenkinson (Australia)
67	5:09.4	Merv Jenkinson (Australia)
	5:26.9	Norman Bright (Washington)
68	5:13.1	Merv Jenkinson (Australia)
	5:24.0	Sydney Madden (California)
69	5:26.3	Otto Essig (Massachusetts)
70	5:30.8	Harold Chapson (Hawaii)

Age	Time	Name
71	5:26.1 N	Reginald Barlow (Australia)
72	5:30.4	Harold Chapson (Hawaii)
73	5:21.5	Harold Chapson (Hawaii)
74	5:21.1	Harold Chapson (Hawaii)
75	5:26.3	Harold Chapson (Hawaii)
76	5:30.1	Harold Chapson (Hawaii)
77	6:27.0	Lou Gregory (Florida)
78	6:28.4	Paul Spangler (California)
79	6:37.2	Paul Spangler (California)
	6:38.0	Paul Spangler (California)

ONE MILE

Age	Time	Name
35	4:03.7	George Scott (New Zealand; California)
	4:21.4 N	Alan Beardall (Oregon)
36	4:24.0	Bill Gookin (California)
37	4:21.5 N	Glynn Wood (Washington DC)
38	4:08.8	George Scott (New Zealand; California)
	4:15.0 N	Glynn Wood (Washington DC)
39	4:13.0 N	Fred Norris (Great Britain)
	4:17.4 N	Glynn Wood (Washington DC)
40	4:21.5	Fred Norris (Great Britain)
	4:24.3	Wilbur Williams (California)
	4:24.3	Glynn Wood (Washington DC)
41	4:21.5	Laurie O'Hara (Great Britain)
	4:28.3 N	Peter Mundle (California)
42	4:26.7 I	Glynn Wood (Washington DC)
	P4:25.0	Kevin Fisher (Australia)
43	4:18.5	Jim McDonald (New Zealand)
	4:24.0	Ray Hatton (Oregon)
44	4:28.0 N	Bill Fitzgerald (California)
45	4:32.0	Denny Meyer (Washington)
46	4:29.5 N	Bill Fitzgerald (California)
47	4:34.5 N	Bill Fitzgerald (California)
48	4:32.8 N	Bill Fitzgerald (California)
49	4:37.7	Bill Fitzgerald (California)
50	4:32.2 N	Bill Fitzgerald (California)
51	4:51.9 NI	George Sheehan (New Jersey)
52	4:53.5 NI	George Sheehan (New Jersey)
53	5:00.7	Avery Bryant (California)
54	4:49.8	Mauro Hernandes (California)
55	4:40.4	Jack Ryan (Australia)
	5:02.2	George Sheehan (New Jersey)
56	5:08.5	Wilson Vible (Delaware)
57	5:04.9	George McGrath (Australia)
	5:06.4	Robert Dellwo (Washington)
58	5:16.0 N	Ray Gordon (Washington DC)
59	5:13.5 N	Clive Davies (Oregon)
60	5:18.8	William Andberg (Minnesota)
61	5:16.8	Clive Davies (Oregon)
62	5:27.2 I	Austin Newman (New Jersey)
63	5:38.0	Norman Bright (Washington)
	P5:32.5	Percy Cerutty (Australia)
64	5:25.4	Stan Nicholls (Australia)
	5:36.4 N	Norman Bright (Washington)
	P5:30.0	Joie Ray (United States)
65	5:22.0 N	Monty Montgomery (California)
66	5:37.2	Stan Nicholls (Australia)
	5:39.5	Norman Bright (Washington)
67	5:41.4	Norman Bright (Washington)
68	5:56.5 N	Sydney Madden (California)
69	5:54.2	Otto Essig (Massachusetts)
70	5:42.2	Monty Montgomery (California)
71	5:54.0 N	Harold Chapson (Hawaii)
72	5:52.3	Harold Chapson (Hawaii)
73	5:51.7	Harold Chapson (Hawaii)
74	6:33.0	Lou Gregory (Florida)
75	7:12.0 I	Lou Gregory (Florida)
76	7:12.0	Lou Gregory (Florida)
77	6:54.0	Paul Spangler (California)
78	7:52.0	Paul Spangler (California)
79	6:59.4	Paul Spangler (California)

3000 METERS

Age	Time	Athlete
35	7:56.2 N	Michel Bernard (France)
	8:37.6 Y	George Young (Arizona)
36	7:57.6 N	Mohamed Gamoudi (Tunisia)
	8:41.8 Y	George Young (Arizona)
37	8:01.2	Gaston Roelants (Belgium)
	9:10.8	Jim Murphy (California)
38	8:13.4	Michel Bernard (France)
	8:58.2	Jim Murphy (California)
39	8:02.2 N	Michel Bernard (France)
	8:58.0 N	Peter Mundle (California)
40	8:25.2	Michel Bernard (France)
	9:00.6	Ray Hatton (Oregon)
41	8:22.0	Alain Mimoun (France)
	9:08.4	Laurie O'Hara (Great Britain)
42	8:24.8	Hal Higdon (Indiana)
	8:52.2	Laurie O'Hara (Great Britain)
43	8:17.4 N	Ray Hatton (Oregon)
	9:26.0	Jack Foster (New Zealand)
44	8:50.0	John Weldy (Arizona)
	8:36.0	Hal Higdon (Indiana)
45	9:20.8	Laurie O'Hara (Great Britain)
	8:52.0 N	Jerry Smartt (United States; Iran)
46	9:14.2	Manuel Alonso (Spain)
	8:46.8	Peter Mundle (California)
47	9:45.8 NY	Manual Alonso (Spain)
	8:57.6	Peter Mundle (California)
48	9:21.4	Manual Alonso (Spain)
	9:06.0 I	George Vernosky (Maryland)
49	9:30.2	Arthur Taylor (Canada)
	9:10.0 I	Peter Mundle (California)
50	9:30.8	Arthur Taylor (Canada)
	9:22.2	Peter Mundle (California)
51	10:09.0	Theo Orr (Australia)
	9:41.4 N	Bob Bartling (South Dakota)
52	9:58.2	Basil Nielsen (Great Britain)
		Jim Forshee (Michigan)
53	9:44.6 N	Mauro Hernandes (California)
54	9:26.0 N	George McGrath (Australia)
55	9:53.0	Mauro Hernandes (California)
	9:12.8	Jack Ryan (Australia)
56	10:39.0	Norman Hansen (Washington)
	9:21.0	John Gilmour (Australia)
57	10:52.8	John Lafferty (California)
	10:19.8 N	Robert Horman (Australia; Washington DC)
	11:17.0 NY	Ed Preston (California)
	11:17.0 Y	Robert Dellwo (Washington)
58	P11:08.2	Rudy Nimmons (United States)
	10:52.0	Cliff Bould (Australia)
59	11:21.4	Danforth Geer (Vermont)
	10:37.6	Thedde Jensen (Sweden)
60	11:14.0 Y	Clive Davies (Oregon)
	11:01.6	Riza Isman (Turkey)
61	11:41.0 NY	John Wall (Maryland)
	10:51.8 N	Riza Isman (Turkey)
62	P10:12.4	Gunter Thiele (West Germany)
	11:28.0 Y	Norman Bright (Washington)
63	10:26.8	Erich Kruzycki (West Germany)
	11:39.4	Bud Deacon (Hawaii)
64	10:41.0	Stan Nicholls (Australia)
	11:38.2	Norman Bright (Washington)
65	10:47.0	William Andberg (Minnesota)
	10:51.0	Norman Bright (Washington)
66	10:47.8	Stan Nicholls (Australia)
	11:30.0 NY	Monty Montgomery (California)
67	11:34.6	Norman Bright (Washington)
68	11:51.0 I	Richard Bredenbeck (Ohio)
69	12:18.0	Victor Blanco (Spain)
	12:41.0	Sydney Madden (California)
70	12:00.2	Reginald Barlow (Australia)
	13:10.0 Y	Richard Bredenbeck (Ohio)
71	12:11.8	Tom Roberts (Georgia)
72	11:55.8 I	Richard Bredenbeck (Ohio)
73	11:46.2	Harold Chapson (Hawaii)
74	12:23.8	Harold Chapson (Hawaii)

Age	Time	Name
75	13:13.8	Lou Gregory (Florida)
76	15:19.8 Y	Paul Spangler (California)
77	14:25.0	Paul Spangler (California)
78	15:41.0 Y	Paul Spangler (California)

2 MILES

Age	Time	Name
35	8:37.2 N	Dave Power (Australia)
	8:37.6 I	George Young (Arizona)
	8:41.8 I	George Young (Arizona)
36	8:57.0	Fred Norris (Great Britain)
37	9:24.0 N	Peter Mundle (California)
	P9:00.4 NI	Frank Pflaging (Maryland)
38	9:41.6	Jim Murphy (California)
39	9:00.0 NI	Fred Norris (Great Britain)
	9:22.0 N	Glynn Wood (Washington DC)
	P9:19.6 NI	Frank Pflaging (Maryland)
40	9:07.4	Fred Norris (Great Britain)
	9:17.6 N	Ray Hatton (Oregon)
41	9:38.8	Peter Mundle (California)
42	9:27.6	Hal Higdon (Indiana)
43	9:19.2	Jim McDonald (New Zealand)
	9:32.8 I	Peter Mundle (California)
44	9:41.0	Hal Higdon (Indiana)
45	9:37.8	Denny Meyer (Washington)
46	9:44.6	Peter Mundle (California)
47	9:45.8 N	Peter Mundle (California)
48	10:24.0	Wayne Hanson (Louisiana)
49	10:07.4	Peter Mundle (California)
50	10:26.0	Peter Mundle (California)
51	10:47.8 N	Mauro Hernandes (California)
52	10:53.6	Leon Dreher (Pennsylvania)
53	10:12.0	George McGrath (Australia)
	10:38.4	Mauro Hernandes (California)
54	10:31.2	Mauro Hernandes (California)
55	10:57.0	Leon Dreher (Pennsylvania)
56	10:07.0	John Gilmour (Australia)
	10:59.2	Leon Dreher (Pennsylvania)
57	11:17.0 N	Ed Preston (California)
	11:17.0	Robert Dellwo (Washington)
58	11:32.0 N	Ray Gordon (Washington DC)
59	11:14.0	Clive Davies (Oregon)
60	11:41.0 N	John Wall (Maryland)
61	11:28.0	Norman Bright (Washington)
62	11:09.0	Don Longenecker (New Mexico)
63	11:52.6	Norman Bright (Washington)
64	11:41.2 N	Norman Bright (Washington)
65	11:35.6	Norman Bright (Washington)
66	11:30.0 N	Monty Montgomery (California)
67	12:36.0	Norman Bright (Washington)
68	12:40.0	Otto Essig (Massachusetts)
69	12:57.4	Otto Essig (Massachusetts)
70	12:47.6	Reginald Barlow (Australia)
	13:10.0 I	Richard Bredenbeck (Ohio)
71	13:09.0 N	Harold Chapson (Hawaii)
72	12:48.0 I.	Richard Bredenbeck (Ohio)
73	12:41.0	Harold Chapson (Hawaii)
74	16:16.9	Lou Gregory (Alabama)
75	15:46.4	Paul Spangler (California)
76	14:30.0	Lou Gregory (Florida)
77	14:41.0	Paul Spangler (California)
78	15:41.0	Paul Spangler (California)

THREE MILES

Age	Time	Name
35	13:30.4 M	Nikolay Sviridov (USSR)
	13:44.2	Peter McArdle (New York)
36	13:38.6 MN	Lucien Rault (France)
	15:11.8	William Hall (North Carolina)
37	P13:54.2 NI	Frank Pflaging (Maryland)
	13:31.6	Gaston Roelants (Belgium)
	14:38.4 N	Peter Mundle (California)

38	13:47.8 MN	Michel Bernard (France)
	15:01.0	Jim Murphy (California)
	P14:36.0 N	Frank Pflaging (Maryland)
39	13:40.0 MN	Michel Bernard (France)
	14:38.0 N	Peter Mundle (California)
40	14:10.2 M	David Francis (Great Britain)
	14:37.0	Ray Hatton (Oregon)
41	14:20.4 M	Gilbert Gauthier (France)
	14:51.8	Peter Mundle (California)
42	14:07.0 M	Jack Foster (New Zealand)
	14:29.2	Ray Hatton (Oregon)
43	14:21.0 M	Jack Foster (New Zealand)
	14:41.6	Ray Hatton (Oregon)
44	14:45.2	Hal Higdon (Indiana)
45	14:56.4 N	Alain Mimoun (France)
	15:32.6	Peter Mundle (California)
46	15:07.0	Peter Mundle (California)
47	15:03.4 M	Manuel Alonso (Spain)
	15:28.0	Peter Mundle (California)
48	15:22.6 M	Manual Alonso (Spain)
	16:04.6 M	George Vernosky (Maryland)
49	15:52.4	Peter Mundle (California)
50	15:31.0 M	Alain Mimoun (France)
	15:37.8	James O'Neil (California)
51	16:12.0 M	Theo Orr (Australia)
	16:14.0 M	James O'Neil (California)
52	15:54.0 M	Jack Ryan (Australia)
	16:12.4	James O'Neil (California)
53	16:05.8 M	John Gilmour (Australia)
	16:22.0	Leon Dreher (Pennsylvania)
54	16:11.0 M	George McGrath (Australia)
	16:49.4	Leon Dreher (Pennsylvania)
55	15:52.8 M	Jack Ryan (Australia)
	17:03.0 M	Mauro Hernandes (California)
56	15:57.0	John Gilmour (Australia)
	17:06.4 M	Leon Dreher (Pennsylvania)
57	16:31.0 M	John Gilmour (Australia)
	17:26.6	James Oleson (California)
58	16:29.0 M	John Gilmour (Australia)
	17:42.2 M	Ed Preston (California)
59	16:51.2	Clive Davies (Oregon)
60	17:42.6 M	William Andberg (Minnesota)
61	17:38.0 M	Clive Davies (Oregon)
62	16:59.2	Don Longenecker (New Mexico)
63	18:15.0 M	Stan Nicholls (Australia)
	18:19.4 N	Norman Bright (Washington)
	18:44.6 M	William Andberg (Minnesota)
65	17:59.2	Norman Bright (Washington)
66	18:00.2	Norman Bright (Washington)
67	18:44.0	Norman Bright (Washington)
68	19:04.2 M	Thedde Jensen (Sweden)
	20:24.0 N	Richard Bredenbeck (Ohio)
69	19:31.0 N	Otto Essig (Massachusetts)
70	20:14.0 M	Syd Hesketh (Australia)
	20:31.0	Richard Bredenbeck (Ohio)
71	19:59.4 M	Einar Nordin (Sweden)
	21:55.0 M	Richard Bredenbeck (Ohio)
72	20:14.4	Harold Chapson (Hawaii)
73	21:39.0 M	Lou Gregory (Alabama)
74	20:38.2	Harold Chapson (Hawaii)
75	20:57.6 M	Louis Charbonneau (France)
	21:10.8	Lou Gregory (Florida)
76	21:54.0	Lou Gregory (Florida)
77	22:16.0 M	Paul Spangler (California)
78	23:24.0 M	Paul Spangler (California)
79	23:53.8 M	Paul Spangler (California)

5000 METERS

35	13:30.4	Nikolay Sviridov (USSR)
	14:17.2	Peter McArdle (New York)
36	13:38.6 N	Lucien Rault (France)
	15:16.0 N	Ray Hughes (California)
37	13:44.4	Gaston Roelants (Belgium)
	15:38.0	Jim Murphy (California)

Age	Time	Name
38	13:47.8 N	Michel Bernard (France)
	15:31.0	Jim Murphy (California)
39	13:40.0 N	Michel Bernard (France)
	15:22.2	Jerry Smartt (United States; Iran)
40	13:45.8	Lucien Rault (France)
	15:26.6	Denny Meyer (Washington)
41	14:20.4	Gilbert Gauthier (France)
	14:59.6 N	Hal Higdon (Indiana)
42	14:07.0	Jack Foster (New Zealand)
	15:09.0	Ray Hatton (Oregon)
43	14:21.0	Jack Foster (New Zealand)
	15:30.8	Jerry Smartt (United States; Iran)
44	14:48.8	Roy Fowler (Great Britain)
	15:09.6	Ray Hatton (Oregon)
45	14:56.4	Alain Mimoun (France)
	15:53.6	Ray Hatton (Oregon)
46	15:36.8 N	Peter Mundle (California)
	15:07.4	Alain Mimoun (France)
47	15:03.4	Manuel Alonso (Spain)
	15:55.8	Peter Mundle (California)
48	15:22.6	Manuel Alonso (Spain)
	16:04.6	George Vernosky (Maryland)
49	15:58.0	Jack Brown (Great Britain)
	16:14.2	Peter Mundle (California)
50	15:31.0	Alain Mimoun (France)
	16:19.6 N	James O'Neil (California)
51	16:03.6	Emil Schulz (West Germany)
	16:14.0	James O'Neil (California)
52	15:54.0	Jack Ryan (Australia)
	16:15.4	James O'Neil (California)
53	16:05.8	John Gilmour (Australia)
	17:01.8 N	Mauro Hernandes (California)
54	16:11.0	George McGrath (Australia)
	17:20.0 N	Leon Dreher (Pennsylvania)
55	15:52.8	Jack Ryan (Australia)
	17:03.0	Mauro Hernandes (California)
56	15:57.0	George McGrath (Australia)
	17:06.4	Leon Dreher (Pennsylvania)
57	16:31.0	John Gilmour (Australia)
	17:40.0 N	Ed Preston (California)
58	16:29.0	John Gilmour (Australia)
59	17:42.2	Ed Preston (California)
	17:22.2	Karl Hasler (Switzerland)
60	18:03.8	James Oleson (California)
61	17:42.6	William Andberg (Minnesota)
62	17:38.0	Clive Davies (Oregon)
	17:23.0	Erich Kruzycki (West Germany)
63	17:35.0	Don Longenecker (New Mexico)
	17:37.6	Clive Davies (Oregon)
64	18:44.6	William Andberg (Minnesota)
	18:04.6	Erich Kruzycki (West Germany)
65	18:33.4	Norman Bright (Washington)
	18:33.0	William Andberg (Minnesota)
66	18:10.0	Stan Nicholls (Australia)
	18:34.2	Norman Bright (Washington)
67	19:21.2	Norman Bright (Washington)
	P19:03.6	G. Helber (West Germany)
68	19:04.2	Thedde Jensen (Sweden)
	20:26.0 N	Otto Essig (Massachusetts)
69	19:43.0	Syd Hesketh (Australia)
	20:23.0 N	Otto Essig (Massachusetts)
70	20:05.4	Ray Sears (Indiana)
71	19:59.4	Einar Nordin (Sweden)
	21:55.0	Richard Bredenbeck (Ohio)
72	20:51.6	Harold Chapson (Hawaii)
73	21:39.0	Reginald Barlow (Australia)
	21:39.0	Lou Gregory (Alabama)
74	21:00.0	Attilio Rossetti (France)
	21:08.0	Lou Gregory (Alabama)
75	20:57.6	Louis Charbonneau (France)
	21:53.0	Lou Gregory (Florida)
76	23:30.0 N	Paul Spangler (California)
77	22:16.0	Paul Spangler (California)
78	23:24.0	Paul Spangler (California)
79	23:53.8	Paul Spangler (California)

SIX MILES

Age	Time	Name
35	27:32.8 N	Jim Hogan (Great Britain)
	28:02.4	Peter McArdle (New York)
36	28:00.4 M	Mariano Haro (Spain)
	29:13.4	Frank Pflaging (Maryland)
37	28:24.8 M	Gaston Roelants (Belgium)
	28:47.4	Oscar Moore (New Jersey)
38	28:14.2 M	Mohamed Gammoudi (Tunisia)
	31:55.2	Michael Tymn (Hawaii)
	P30:56.0 MN	Frank Pflaging (Maryland)
39	28:46.8 M	Jack Foster (New Zealand)
	30:52.6	Denny Meyer (Washington)
	P30:27.0	Frank Pflaging (Maryland)
40	28:33.4 M	Lucien Rault (France)
	30:44.0	Ray Hatton (Oregon)
41	28:50.4 M	Lucien Rault (France)
	30:26.2	Hal Higdon (Indiana)
42	29:11.4 M	Jack Foster (New Zealand)
	30:10.4	Hal Higdon (Indiana)
43	29:57.4 MN	Alain Mimoun (France)
	29:59.0	Ray Hatton (Oregon)
44	29:29.6 N	Charles Smart (Great Britain)
	32:00.0 M	Ray Hatton (Oregon)
45	30:16.8 M	Alain Mimoun (France)
	30:47.0	Ray Hatton (Oregon)
46	31:29.0	Peter Mundle (California)
47	30:47.0 M	Alain Mimoun (France)
	32:19.6 N	Peter Mundle (California)
48	32:13.2 M	Manual Alonso (Spain)
	33:40.0 MN	James O'Neil (California)
49	31:33.8 M	Alain Mimoun (France)
	33:51.0 M	Peter Mundle (California)
50	32:30.4 M	Alain Mimoun (France)
	32:40.0	Peter Mundle (California)
51	32:14.0 M	Alain Mimoun (France)
	33:07.0	James O'Neil (California)
52	32:36.2 M	Alain Mimoun (France)
53	33:14.0	James O'Neil (California)
	33:05.0 M	John Gilmour (Australia)
54	34:56.0	Leon Dreher (Pennsylvania)
	34:25.6 M	Kenneth Hall (Great Britain)
55	35:27.0 M	Gerald Morrison (Missouri)
	33:40.0 M	John Gilmour (Australia)
	35:08.0	Leon Dreher (Pennsylvania)
56	33:44.2 M	John Gilmour (Australia)
	35:37.2 M	Leon Dreher (Pennsylvania)
57	33:40.8 M	John Gilmour (Australia)
	36:02.2	Ed Preston (California)
58	33:58.0 M	John Gilmour (Australia)
	36:02.0	Ed Preston (California)
59	35:05.0	Clive Davies (Oregon)
60	36:16.0 M	Robert McMinnis (Great Britain)
	36:23.0 MN	Clive Davies (Oregon)
61	35:57.4 M	Erich Kruzycki (West Germany)
	36:49.2	Norman Bright (Washington)
62	37:08.0 M	William Andberg (Minnesota)
63	35:19.8 M	Clive Davies (Oregon)
64	37:42.0 M	Thedde Jensen (Sweden)
	41:02.2 M	Bob Boal (North Carolina)
65	36:04.6 MN	Thedde Jensen (Sweden)
	38:17.4 N	Norman Bright (Washington)
66	36:55.8	Stan Nicholls (Australia)
	37:24.4	Norman Bright (Washington)
67	40:42.0 M	Hans Mohr (West Germany)
	40:58.2 M	Norman Bright (Washington)
68	39:16.0 M	Thedde Jensen (Sweden)
	41:13.0 MN	Otto Essig (Massachusetts)
69	40:50.0 M	Ray Sears (Indiana)
70	41:21.0 M	Ray Sears (Indiana)
71	40:48.6 M	Einar Nordin (Sweden)
	45:56.0	Richard Bredenbeck (Ohio)
72	43:11.0	Harold Chapson (Hawaii)
73	42:38.0	Fred Grace (California)

Age	Time	Name
48	32:13.2	Manuel Alonso (Spain)
	33:40.0 N	James O'Neil (California)
49	31:33.8	Alain Mimoun (France)
	33:51.0	Peter Mundle (California)
50	32:30.4	Alain Mimoun (France)
	33:53.0	Peter Mundle (California)
51	32:14.0	Alain Mimoun (France)
	33:30.0	James O'Neil (California)
52	32:36.2	Alain Mimoun (France)
	33:40.2	James O'Neil (California)
53	33:05.0	John Gilmour (Australia)
	33:46.0	James O'Neil (California)
54	34:25.6	Kenneth Hall (Great Britain)
	35:27.0	Gerald Morrison (Missouri)
55	33:40.0	John Gilmour (Australia)
	35:38.0	Gerald Morrison (Missouri)
56	33:44.2	John Gilmour (Australia)
	35:37.2	Leon Dreher (Pennsylvania)
57	33:40.8	John Gilmour (Australia)
	36:39.0	Ed Preston (California)
58	33:58.0	John Gilmour (Australia)
	37:04.0	Ed Preston (California)
59	34:52.8	John Gilmour (Australia)
	38:09.8	James Oleson (California)
60	36:16.0	Robert McMinnis (Great Britain)
	36:23.0 N	Clive Davies (Oregon)
61	35:57.4 N	Erich Kruzycki (West Germany)
	37:34.4 N	Norman Bright (Washington)
62	37:08.0	William Andberg (Minnesota)
63	35:19.8	Clive Davies (Oregon)
64	37:42.0	Thedde Jensen (Sweden)
	41:02.2	Bob Boal (North Carolina)
65	36:04.6 N	Thedde Jensen (Sweden)
	38:48.0 N	William Andberg (Minnesota)
66	37:52.2	Stan Nicholls (Australia)
	38:38.0	Norman Bright (Washington)
67	40:42.0	Hans Mohr (West Germany)
	40:58.2	Norman Bright (Washington)

Age	Time	Name
74	44:16.2 M	Louis Charbonneau (France)
	46:15.0 M	Lou Gregory (Alabama)
75	42:34.8 M	Luis Rivera (Mexico)
	48:43.0 M	Lou Gregory (Florida)
76	44:35.0	Lou Gregory (Florida)
77	45:53.4	Paul Spangler (California)
78	47:16.6	Paul Spangler (California)
79	48:19.0 M	Paul Spangler (California)

10,000 METERS

Age	Time	Name
35	27:58.6	Nikolay Sviridov (USSR)
	29:03.4	Peter McArdle (New York)
36	28:00.4	Mariano Haro (Spain)
	30:47.8 N	Ray Hughes (California)
37	28:24.8	Gaston Roelants (Belgium)
	32:57.0 N	Peter Mundle (California)
38	28:14.2	Mohamed Gammoudi (Tunisia)
	30:52.6	Ray Hughes (California)
39	28:46.8	Jack Foster (New Zealand)
	31:48.0	Jerry Smartt (United States; Iran)
40	28:33.4	Lucien Rault (France)
	31:42.8	Ray Hatton (Oregon)
41	28:50.4 N	Lucien Rault (France)
	31:18.4	Hal Higdon (Indiana)
42	29:11.4	Jack Foster (New Zealand)
	31:09.2 N	Hal Higdon (Indiana)
43	29:57.4 N	Alain Mimoun (France)
	30:56.0	Ray Hatton (Oregon)
44	30:32.6	Alain Mimoun (France)
	32:00.0	Ray Hatton (Oregon)
45	30:16.8	Alain Mimoun (France)
	31:48.0	Ray Hatton (Oregon)
46	31:50.0	Dave Power (Australia)
	32:30.8 N	Peter Mundle (California)
47	30:47.0	Alain Mimoun (France)
	33:19.0	George Vernosky (Maryland)

No.	Age	Distance	Name
43	11M	420Y	Ron Franklin (Great Britain)
44	11M	187Y	Denny Meyer (Washington)
45	11M	740Y	Ray Hatton (Oregon)
	11M	1268Y	Alain Mimoun (France)
46	10M	1554Y	Dick Bartek (California)
	10M	1663Y	Walter Weba (West Germany)
	10M	1520Y	Peter Mundle (California)
47	11M	844Y	Alain Mimoun (France)
	10M	1212Y	James McDonagh (New York)
48	10M	512Y	Bob Bartling (South Dakota)
49	11M	816Y	Alain Mimoun (France)
	10M	614Y	Peter Mundle (California)
50	11M	954Y	Alain Mimoun (France)
	10M	1335Y	Peter Mundle (California)
51	11M	369Y	Alain Mimoun (France)
	10M	273Y	Ed Keysar (California)
	10M	385Y	Cliff Bould (Australia)
52	10M	232Y	James McDonagh (New York)
53	10M	147Y	Ed Almeida (California)
54	10M	385Y	Cliff Bould (Australia)
	9M	1700Y	Leon Dreher (Pennsylvania)
	P10M	263Y	Hubert Morgan (Pennsylvania)
55	10M	1194Y	John Gilmour (Australia)
	10M	279Y	Hubert Morgan (Pennsylvania)
56	10M	215Y	Leon Dreher (Pennsylvania)
57	9M	885Y	John Lafferty (California)
58	10M	910Y	John Gilmour (Australia)
	9M	473Y	Wayne Zook (California)
59	10M	932Y	John Gilmour (Australia)
	9M	1535Y	Clive Davies (Oregon)
60	9M	880Y	William Andberg (Minnesota)
61	10M	201Y	Clive Davies (Oregon)
62	9M	98Y	Bob Boal (North Carolina)
63	9M	478Y	Norman Bright (Washington)
	P 9M	1214Y	Bouder (France)
64	8M	1364Y	Bob Boal (North Carolina)
65	9M	604Y	Norman Bright (Washington)
66	9M	360Y	Norman Bright (Washington)

No.	Time	Name
68	39:16.0	Thedde Jensen (Sweden)
69	41:13.0 N	Otto Essig (Massachusetts)
70	40:50.0	Ray Sears (Indiana)
71	41:21.0	Ray Sears (Indiana)
	40:48.6	Einar Nordin (Sweden)
72	46:27.2	Harold Keith (Oklahoma)
73	44:31.2	Harold Chapson (Hawaii)
	45:47.0	Reginald Barlow (Australia)
74	47:26.0	Lou Gregory (Alabama)
	44:16.2	Louis Charbonneau (France)
	46:15.0	Lou Gregory (Alabama)
75	42:34.8	Luis Rivera (Mexico)
	48:43.0	Lou Gregory (Florida)
76	45:10.0	Luis Rivera (Mexico)
	46:27.0	Lou Gregory (Florida)
77	47:30.0 N	Paul Spangler (California)
78	47:23.0	Paul Spangler (California)
79	48:19.0	Paul Spangler (California)

ONE-HOUR RUN

No.	Age	Distance	Name
35	12M	1599Y	Gaston Roelants (Belgium)
	11M	1070Y	Ken Mueller (Massachusetts)
36	12M	441Y	Josef Jansky (Czechoslovakia)
	11M	1065Y	Ken Mueller (Massachusetts)
37	12M	1086Y	Lucien Rault (France)
	11M	720Y	Dave Waco (California)
38	12M	788Y	Lucien Rault (France)
	11M	600Y	Peter Mundle (California)
39	11M	642Y	Denny Meyer (Washington)
	P11M	907Y	Maurice Simonit (France)
40	11M	1309Y	William Stoddart (Great Britain)
	11M	540Y	Ken Mueller (Massachusetts)
41	11M	677Y	Hal Higdon (Indiana)
42	11M	793Y	Ron Franklin (Great Britain)
	11M	340Y	John Brennand (California)

Age	Mark	Name
67	8M 1238Y	Norman Bright (Washington)
68	8M 225Y	Richard Bredenbeck (Ohio)
69	8M 672Y	Otto Essig (Massachusetts)
	P 8M 990Y	Ray Sears (Indiana)
70	8M 692Y	Reginald Barlow (Australia)
	8M 664Y	Richard Bredenbeck (Ohio)
71	7M 1101Y	Richard Bredenbeck (Ohio)
72	6M 56Y	Curtis Wright (Pennsylvania)
73	8M 394Y	Louis Charbonneau (France)
	6M 156Y	Curtis Wright (Pennsylvania)
74	7M 962Y	Paul Spangler (California)
75	8M 335Y	Lou Gregory (Florida)
76	7M 131Y	Lou Gregory (Florida)
77	7M 889Y	Paul Spangler (California)
78	7M 1735Y	Paul Spangler (California)

Age	Mark	Name
44	2:17:54	Jack Foster (New Zealand)
	2:34:11	John J. Kelley (Connecticut)
45	2:22:06	Jack Foster (New Zealand)
	2:29:07 N	James McDonagh (New York)
46	2:17:29	Jack Foster (New Zealand)
	2:28:49 N	James McDonagh (New York)
47	2:20:54.6	Erik Ostbye (Sweden)
	2:30:26	Hal Higdon (Indiana)
48	2:23:56	Erik Ostbye (Sweden)
	2:37:49	Howard Miller (Washington)
49	2:24:34	Erik Ostbye (Sweden)
	2:37:30	James McDonagh (New York)
50	2:27:17	Arthur Taylor (Canada)
	2:38:04	Ross Smith (Nevada)
51	2:25:19	Erik Ostbye (Sweden)
	2:35:48	James O'Neil (California)
52	2:31:30	Erik Ostbye (Sweden)
	2:35:43	Alex Ratelle (Minnesota)
53	2:29:20	Erik Ostbye (Sweden)
	2:31:56	Alex Ratelle (Minnesota)
54	2:34:43	Erik Ostbye (Sweden)
	2:36:09	Alex Ratelle (Minnesota)
55	2:26:35	Erik Ostbye (Sweden)
	2:41:27	Ed Almeida (California)
56	2:27:05	Erik Ostbye (Sweden)
	2:45:13	Ed Almeida (California)
57	2:48:32	John A. Kelley (Massachusetts)
58	2:50:14	John Gilmour (Australia)
	2:51:44 N	William Andberg (Minnesota)
59	2:38:19	John Gilmour (Australia)
	2:52:29	Clive Davies (Oregon)
60	2:47:46	Clive Davies (Oregon)
61	2:50:54	Clive Davies (Oregon)
62	2:49:17	Clive Davies (Oregon)
63	2:53:28	Clive Davies (Oregon)
64	2:55:45	Monty Montgomery (California)
65	2:53:03 N	Monty Montgomery (California)
66	2:56:45 N	Monty Montgomery (California)

MARATHON

Age	Time	Name
35	2:13:12	Terry Manners (New Zealand)
	2:15:52 N	Norman Higgins (Connecticut)
36	2:12:35	Ron Hill (Great Britain)
	2:17:43	Herb Lorenz (Pennsylvania)
37	2:13:44	Alastair Wood (Great Britain)
	2:24:54	Ken Mueller (Massachusetts)
38	2:12:17.8	Jack Foster (New Zealand)
	2:20:21	Edwin Fry (Pennsylvania)
39	2:13:42.4	Jack Foster (New Zealand)
	2:24:38	Fred Best (New Jersey)
40	P2:23:30	Ralph Thomas (Maine)
	2:24:41	Herb Lorenz (New Jersey)
41	2:27:56	Ken Mueller (Massachusetts)
	2:11:18.6	Jack Foster (New Zealand)
42	2:20:47	Fritz Mueller (New York)
	2:18:24	Jack Foster (New Zealand)
	2:25:21	Fritz Mueller (New York)
43	2:16:07	Jack Foster (New Zealand)
	2:29:23	John Brennand (California)

Age	Time	Name
67	3:07:35	Thedde Jensen (Sweden)
68	3:11:11	Norman Bright (Washington)
69	2:54:49	Monty Montgomery (California)
70	3:00:57	Monty Montgomery (California)
	3:08:45	Einar Nordin (Sweden)
	P3:06:24	Wally Hayward (South Africa)
71	3:15:45	Monty Montgomery (California)
72	3:07:03	Monty Montgomery (California)
73	3:14:47	Monty Montgomery (California)
	4:02:55	George Vang (Norway)
74	4:03:38	Fred Grace (California)
	3:40:28	Friedrich Tempel (West Germany)
	3:45:15	Fred Grace (California)
75	3:31:42	Friedrich Tempel (West Germany)
	3:47:20	Lou Gregory (Alabama)
76	3:36:27	Friedrich Tempel (West Germany)
	3:53:29	Lou Gregory (Florida)
77	4:20:51	Fred Grace (California)
78	3:52:50	Arthur Lambert (West Germany)
	4:06:20	Paul Spangler (California)
79	3:59:47	Paul Spangler (California)
80	P4:56:28	Josef Galia (West Germany)
	P5:21:05	A. Neuchel (West Germany)
84	7:35:00	Claude Mulholland (Oregon)
95	P6:42:00	Christos Iordanidis (Greece)
98	P7:33:00	Christos Iordanidis (Greece)

WOMEN'S MASTERS RECORDS

COMPILED BY KATHARINE BRIEGER

100 YARDS

Age	Time	Name
36	12.8	Miriam Gerard (California)
37	13.9	Ursula Schreiber (California)
	P13.0	Betty Parks (United States)
38	12.3	Almeta Parish (California)
39	14.3	Ursula Schreiber (California)
40	13.8	Almeta Parish (California)
	P13.6	Betty Pappas (United States)
41	11.4	Irene Obera (California)
42	11.4	Irene Obera (California)
43	12.6	Irene Obera (California)
44	14.2	Katharine Brieger (California)
45	15.0	Katharine Brieger (California)
47	14.2	Ellen Rose (California)
	14.2	Shirley Kinsey (California)
48	13.3	Ellen Rose (California)
49	14.8	Ellen Rose (California)
50	15.0	Shirley Dietderich (California)
54	16.1	Martha Fairbank (North Carolina)
55	16.0	Martha Fairbank (North Carolina)
59	15.8	Josephine Kolda (California)
60	15.5	Josephine Kolda (California)
63	16.9 W	Polly Clarke (Colorado)
65	16.0	Polly Clarke (Colorado)

100 METERS

Age	Time	Name
35	12.3	Cherrie Sherrard (California)
36	12.2	Cherrie Sherrard (California)
37	12.2	Cherrie Sherrard (California)
38	12.7	Cherrie Sherrard (California)
39	12.5	Cherrie Sherrard (California)
40	13.1	Christel Miller (California)
41	12.8 H	Irene Obera (California)
41	12.5 W	Irene Obera (California)
42	12.6	Irene Obera (California)
43	13.0	Irene Obera (California)
44	15.1	Katharine Brieger (California)
45	15.9	Isabel McConnell (New Jersey)
46	14.5	Ellen Rose (California)
47	15.2	Ellen Rose (California)
48	15.0	Shirley Kinsey (California)
48	15.0	Ellen Rose (California)
49	15.6	Shirley Kinsey (California)
50	15.9	Shirley Dietderich (California)
51	16.2	Shirley Dietderich (California)
52	15.0	Ruth Christian (California)
53	14.8	Ruth Christian (California)
54	16.1	Cathy Hargus (California)
55	17.9	Martha Fairbank (North Carolina)
56	16.5	Martha Fairbank (North Carolina)
57	18.4	Ernestine Yeomans (Ohio)
58	18.5	Ernestine Yeomans (Ohio)
59	17.0	Josephine Kolda (California)
60	16.8	Josephine Kolda (California)
62	16.5	Edith Mendyka (California)
63	18.3	Edith Mendyka (California)
64	18.6	Edith Mendyka (California)
65	18.5	Edith Mendyka (California)
65	17.8 W	Polly Clarke (Colorado)
67	16.1 M	Polly Clarke (Colorado)

200 METERS-220 YARDS

Age	Time	Name
35	26.6 M	Cherrie Sherrard (California)
36	26.0 M	Cherrie Sherrard (California)
37	26.1 M	Ursula Schreiber (California)
38	26.9 M	Cherrie Sherrard (California)
39	26.9 M	Almeta Parish (California)
40	27.5 M	Christel Miller (California)
41	27.3 M	Irene Obera (California)
41	26.3 WM	Irene Obera (California)
42	26.1 M	Irene Obera (California)
43	27.3 M	Irene Obera (California)
44	27.6 M	Irene Obera (California)
45	34.2 M	Nicki Hobson (California)
46	33.4 M	Ellen Rose (California)
47	32.1 WMH	Ellen Rose (California)
48	31.8 M	Ellen Rose (California)
48	31.7 M	Shirley Kinsey (California)
49	31.2 WM	Shirley Kinsey (California)
49	31.5	Ellen Rose (California)
50	29.6	Shirley Dietderich (California)
51	34.7 M	Cathy Hargus (California)
51	33.6 WM	Shirley Dietderich (California)
54	35.5 M	Cathy Hargus (California)
55	40.0 M	Martha Fairbank (North Carolina)
56	37.5 M	Martha Fairbank (North Carolina)
57	39.0 M	Ernestine Yeomans (Ohio)
58	42.6 M	Josephine Kolda (California)
59	38.2	Josephine Kolda (California)
60	37.6 M	Josephine Kolda (California)
62	36.9 WM	Burnis Hicks (Texas)
63	43.0 WMH	Burnis Hicks (Texas)
65	41.0 M	Polly Clarke (Colorado)
65	40.4	Polly Clarke (Colorado)
67	35.1 M	Polly Clarke (Colorado)

400 METERS-440 YARDS

Age	Time	Name
35	61.2 M	Miriam Gerard (California)
36	60.6 M	Miki Hervey (Texas)
37	62.8 M	Almeta Parish (California)
38	62.5 M	Almeta Parish (California)
39	62.3 M	Almeta Parish (California)
40	62.7 M	Almeta Parish (California)
41	61.5 M	Irene Obera (California)
42	59.9 M	Irene Obera (California)
43	62.4 M	Irene Obera (California)
44	64.2 M	Irene Obera (California)
45	76.0 M	Nicki Hobson (California)
46	73.0 M	Jeannette Powell (California)
47	73.4 M	Ellen Rose (California)
48	70.1 M	Ellen Rose (California)
49	70.5 M	Shirley Dietderich (California)
50	80.2 M	Shirley Dietderich (California)
51	81.7 M	Shirley Dietderich (California)
54	94.9 M	Martha Fairbank (North Carolina)
55	88.0 M	Cathy Hargus (California)
56	91.7 M	Martha Fairbank (North Carolina)
57	92.4 M	Ernestine Yeomans (Ohio)
58	97.0 M	Ernestine Yeomans (Ohio)
59	89.2 M	Josephine Kolda (California)
60	91.1 M	Josephine Kolda (California)
62	93.7 M	Burnis Hicks (Texas)
63	89.3 M	Burnis Hicks (Texas)
64	92.8	Polly Clarke (Colorado)
65	84.9 M	Polly Clarke (Colorado)
66	99.9	Polly Clarke (Colorado)
67	83.2 M	Polly Clarke (Colorado)

800 METERS-880 YARDS

Age	Time	Name
36	2:22.2 M	Miki Hervey (Texas)
37	2:33.3 M	Miriam Gerard (California)
38	2:16.5 M	Susan Buchanan (Pennsylvania)
40	2:32.2	Mary Czarapata (Wisconsin)
41	P2:32.2	Almeta Parish (California)
42	2:30.0 M	Mary Czarapata (Wisconsin)
43	2:26.1 M	Mary Czarapata (Wisconsin)
44	2:45.0	Myrrha Eberly (California)
45	2:49.7 M	Nicki Hobson (California)
46	2:40.1	Chris McKenzie (New York)
47	3:05.3 M	Ellen Rose (California)
48	2:46.1 M	Ruth Anderson (California)
49	3:07.0	Ellen Rose (California)
50	3:00.8 M	Jan Newhart (Hawaii)
51	3:42.0 M	Angeline Trantham (Texas)
54	P2:49.1 M	Margaret Miller (California)
55	3:42.0 M	Martha Fairbank (North Carolina)
58	3:28.7 M	Edith Leiby (Hawaii)
60	3:45.0 M	Ernestine Yeomans (Ohio)
61	4:16.1 M	Alice Werbel (California)
63	3:41.3 M	Alice Werbel (California)
64	3:44.6 M	Burnis Hicks (Texas)
67	3:58.0	Polly Clarke (Colorado)
82	3:35.9	Polly Clarke (Colorado)
85	5:47.5 M	Hulda Crooks (California)
86	7:03.0 M	Eula Weaver (California)
87	7:05.0 M	Eula Weaver (California)
88	7:28.6 M	Eula Weaver (California)

1500 METERS

Age	Time	Name
35	4:40.2	Cindy Dalrymple (Hawaii)
36	5:10.0	Barbara Pike (California)
	P5:08.0	Emma Childers (United States)
38	4:46.0	Susan Buchanan (Pennsylvania)
39	5:47.0	Dorothy Stock (California)
	P5:32.7	Rebecca Douglas (United States)

Age	Time	Name
40	5:05.7	Martha Klopfer (North Carolina)
	P5:00.6	Pat Bessel (New York)
41	5:49.0 I	Donna Gookin (California)
42	4:40.0	Miki Gorman (California)
43	5:10.2	Linda Sipprelle (Washington DC)
44	5:56.5	Carol O'Conner (California)
45	5:21.5 I	Dorothy Stock (California)
46	5:18.9 I	Nicki Hobson (California)
47	5:20.1	Ruth Anderson (California)
48	5:30.4	Ruth Anderson (California)
49	5:55.0 I	Ellen Rose (California)
50	6:13.1	Jan Newhart (Hawaii)
51	6:27.0	Cathy Hargus (California)
54	7:23.7	Martha Fairbank (North Carolina)
55	6:05.2	Edith Carlisle (California)
56	6:53.0	Ernestine Yeomans (Ohio)
58	7:17.0	Ernestine Yeomans (Ohio)
59	8:20.6	Josephine Kolda (California)
60	8:29.0	Alice Werbel (California)
62	7:21.0	Burnis Hicks (Texas)
63	7:27.2	Burnis Hicks (Texas)
67	7:34.2	Polly Clarke (Colorado)
85	13:56.8	Eula Weaver (California)
86	13:58.1	Eula Weaver (California)
88	16:34.6	Eula Weaver (California)

MILE

Age	Time	Name
35	5:22.0	Katie McIntyre (California)
36	6:07.1 I	Nina Kuscsik (United States)
37	5:15.5	Susan Buchanan (Pennsylvania)
38	5:27.3	Susan Buchanan (Pennsylvania)
39	5:39.5	Martha Klopper (North Carolina)
40	5:24.0	Pat Bessel (New York)
41	5:16.2	Miki Gorman (California)
42	5:27.8 I	Mary Czarapata (Wisconsin)

Age	Time	Name
43	6:19.5	Ruth Waters (California)
	P6:19.3	Ruth Waters (California)
44	5:46.4	Dorothy Stock (California)
45	5:45.0	Toshiko D'Elia (New Jersey)
46	5:43.0	Toshiko D'Elia (New Jersey)
47	5:52.1	Nicki Hobson (California)
48	5:57.0	Ruth Anderson (California)
49	6:55.1	Cathy Hargus (California)
50	6:31.4	Ruth Dettering (California)
51	5:52.1	Margaret Miller (California)
54	8:10.7	Martha Fairbank (North Carolina)
61	8:08.4	Burnis Hicks (Texas)
65	8:24.0	Polly Clarke (Colorado)
66	8:49.0	Polly Clarke (Colorado)
67	8:19.0	Polly Clarke (Colorado)

3000 METERS

Age	Time	Name
40	P11:23.0	Mary Czarapata (Wisconsin)
41	10:04.0	Miki Gorman (California)
42	11:00.0	Mary Czarapata (Wisconsin)
43	11:38.2 Y	Linda Sipprelle (Washington DC)
44	11:23.2	Dorothy Stock (California)
45	11:35.8	Dorothy Stock (California)
46	12:26.6	Carol O'Conner (California)
47	11:44.0	Nicki Hobson (California)
49	14:24.0	Stella Sharp (California)
55	16:56.8	Martha Fairbank (North Carolina)
61	14:56.0	Alice Werbel (California)

2 MILES

Age	Time	Name
35	12:11.4 I	Sandy Pashkin (New York)
37	P14:04.6	Yvonne Krupp (United States)
39	11:39.6 I	Nina Kuscsik (United States)
40	12:13.0 I	Susan Buchanan (Pennsylvania)
42	11:38.0	Linda Sipprelle (Washington DC)

Age	Time	Name
43	11:38.2	Linda Sipprelle (Washington DC)
44	16:09.2	Isabel McConnell (New Jersey)
45	12:24.4	Nicki Hobson (California)
46	16:52.0 I	Virginia Lucas (United States)

5000 METERS

Age	Time	Name
35	21:54.0	Donna Gookin (California)
	P19:46.6	Betty Wake (California)
36	19:36.6	Barbara Pike (California)
38	18:44.8	Susan Buchanan (Pennsylvania)
39	22:02.0	Dorothy Stock (California)
40	19:17.0	Pat Bessel (New York)
41	16:57.0	Miki Gorman (California)
42	18:54.6	Dorothy Stock (California)
43	18:39.0	Linda Sipprelle (Washington DC)
44	19:18.0	Dorothy Stock (California)
45	18:55.4	Nicki Hobson (California)
46	20:13.0	Ruth Anderson (California)
47	25:36.8	Barbara Barnes (Connecticut)
48	19:57.8	Ruth Anderson (California)
49	25:00.0	Stella Sharp (California)
50	22:34.0	Jan Newhart (Hawaii)
51	23:19.4	Cathy Hargus (California)
55	26:30.0	Edith Carlisle (California)
58	30:09.0	Ruth Osiel (Hawaii)
61	23:22.4	Alice Werbel (California)
62	29:14.6	Burnis Hicks (Texas)
63	28:14.2	Burnis Hicks (Texas)

10,000 METERS

Age	Time	Name
35	36:25.4	Cindy Dalrymple (Hawaii)
36	39:38.2	Skip Swannack (California)
37	41:56.8	Karen Frank (California)
38	P49:29.0	Rebecca Campbell (United States)
40	35:51.0	Miki Gorman (California)
41	39:57.8	Linda Sipprelle (Washington DC)
	P35:50.0	Miki Gorman (California)
42	35:45.6	Miki Gorman (California)
43	40:07.0	Dorothy Stock (California)
44	40:28.2	Dorothy Stock (California)
45	40:19.8	Dorothy Stock (California)
46	40:20.0	Ruth Anderson (California)
47	39:53.0	Toshiko D'Elia (New Jersey)
48	42:06.6	Ruth Anderson (California)
49	47:35.2	Jan Newhart (Hawaii)
50	46:17.0	Jan Newhart (Hawaii)
51	55:55.6	Joan Flynn (Hawaii)
55	53:24.0	Edith Carlisle (California)
59	56:48.0	Alice Werbel (California)
61	53:33.0	Alice Werbel (California)
63	57:52.0	Burnis Hicks (Texas)
67	67:45.0	Ruth Updegrove (Hawaii)

ONE-HOUR RUN

Age	Distance	Name
35	9M 1044Y	Cindy Dalrymple (Hawaii)
36	8M 95Y	Dixie Marquez (Oklahoma)
	9M 1124Y	Marylin Paul (United States)
37	8M 716Y	Martha Klopfer (North Carolina)
	9M 248Y	Marylin Paul (United States)
38	8M 495Y	Donna Gookin (California)
	8M 1110Y	Lolitia Bache (California)
39	8M 1665Y	Martha Klopfer (North Carolina)
40	8M 1536Y	Mary Czarapata (Wisconsin)
41	9M 135Y	Mary Czarapata (Wisconsin)
42	9M 575Y	Linda Sipprelle (Washington DC)
43	9M 1197Y	Linda Sipprelle (Washington DC)
44	7M 10Y	Katie Carey (United States)
	6M 1246Y	Valerie Hanna (Hawaii)
45	8M 1674Y	Nicki Hobson (California)

Age	Distance		Name
46	P8M	1693Y	Ruth Anderson (California)
47	8M	1291Y	Ruth Anderson (California)
48	8M	462Y	Margaret Miller (California)
49	8M	468Y	Margaret Miller (California)
50	8M	144Y	Jean Spierling (California)
51	P6M	626Y	Ruth Sullivan (Missouri)
52	8M	880Y	Margaret Miller (California)
53	P6M	1251Y	Traude Weller (Texas)
	P5M	1596Y	Liz Davies (Washington)
55	7M	752Y	Ernestine Yeomans (Ohio)
56	P7M	434Y	Laurel Henley (United States)
	P5M	510Y	Rachel Harder (California)
58	7M	1021Y	Marcia Trent (Alaska)
59	6M	709Y	Alice Werbel (California)
61	6M	1507Y	Alice Werbel (California)

TWO-HOUR RUN

Age	Distance		Name
40	15M	239Y	Yvonne Livett (California)
43	15M	1399Y	Linda Sipprelle (Washington DC)
45	12M	1041Y	Donna Ferrari (California)
46	14M	1726Y	Carol O'Conner (California)
47	17M	324Y	Ruth Anderson (California)
50	P12M	1645Y	Marie Heissler (United States)
54	10M	1750Y	Annabel Marsh (California)
60	P12M	110Y	Kay Atkinson (United States)

MARATHON

Age	Time	Name
35	2:48:08	Cindy Dalrymple (Hawaii)
36	2:51:15	Joan Ullyot (California)
37	2:58:43	Joan Ullyot (California)
	P2:54:10	Marylin Paul (United States)
38	2:46:36	Miki Gorman (California)
39	2:57:22	Nina Kuscsik (United States)
40	2:47:45	Miki Gorman (California)
41	2:39:11	Miki Gorman (California)
42	2:43:10	Miki Gorman (California)
43	3:12:24	Luanne Dewitt (California)
44	3:05:18	Nicki Hobson (California)
45	2:57:41	Nicki Hobson (California)
46	3:00:14	Nicki Hobson (California)
47	3:04:54	Toshiko D'Elia (New Jersey)
48	3:04:19	Ruth Anderson (California)
49	3:09:58	Ruth Anderson (California)
50	3:10:29	Carol Cartwright (California)
51	3:18:48	Margaret Miller (California)
52	3:14:20	Margaret Miller (California)
53	P4:05:03	Virginia Terry (United States)
54	3:43:37	Marcia Trent (Alaska)
55	4:15:22	Marcia Trent (Alaska)
56	3:50:54	Marcia Trent (Alaska)
57	3:27:45	Marcia Trent (Alaska)
58	3:53:23	Marcia Trent (Alaska)
59	3:34:22	Marcia Trent (Alaska)
60	3:26:16	Marcia Trent (Alaska)
61	4:54:23	Burnis Hicks (Texas)
63	5:11:25	Burnis Hicks (Texas)
64	5:06:01	Burnis Hicks (Texas)
65	4:59:36	Burnis Hicks (Texas)
70	4:45:02	Mavis Lindgren (California)
71	4:38:46	Mavis Lindgren (California)